More Work in Progress

Course Book

Andy Hopkins
Jocelyn Potter

with Madeleine du Vivier

Introduction

More Work in Progress is about people who work in four different companies. Look at the pictures of the companies below.

1 Match each photo (A – D) with the photo and texts (1 – 4) on the opposite page.

2 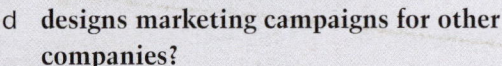 Listen to the tape. Match each extract with one of the companies.

3 Which company:
a is a manufacturer?
b makes and sells television programmes?
c is a large retail organisation?
d designs marketing campaigns for other companies?

1

neuhaus

NEUHAUS STARTER PACK:

Customer: .... Order date: ....

.... Delivery date: ....

.... Agent: ....

Product	Code	Retail Price	Order Qty
Theatre Royal	NB6877	£13.50	3
La Traviata	NB6876	£13.50	3
Tosca	NB6875	£13.50	3
Orangettes	NB6871	£6.95	4
Truffles	NB6830	£6.95	4

2

FLIGHT VUELO	DESTINATION DESTINO	TIME HORA	COUNTER MOSTR.	BOARDING T. H. EMBAR.	GATE PUERTA	REMARKS OBSERVACIONES
CF6 7633	DUSSELDORF	15:15	12-14	14:30		
LX 699	GINEBRA	15:30	9	14:45		
IB 5142	LONDRES HEATH	15:45	1- 8	15:00		
AO 706	BARCELONA	16:00	1- 8	15:30		
FV 8065	PALMA	16:30	17-18	16:00		
AO 645	MADRID	18:10	1- 8	17:40		
LTU 147	DUSSELDORF	18:15	10-12	17:30		
UX 1916	PALMA	18:20	21-22	17:50		

3

THE PROGRAMMES

Special Music Shows

● **Club MTV**
the best club in Europe comes to your front room

● **Unplugged**
the show that put a new word in the dictionary and a new chapter in musical history

● **StarTrax**
the stars reveal their favourite music

● **Amour**
a one hour mix of the most sensuous, seductive love songs around

4

intra

SOME OF OUR CLIENTS

Arla (Sweden's largest dairy product company), Telia (Telecom company) Saab Combitech Network, Nokia Display Products, Q8 Kuwait Petroleum, Uppsala Energi, TCM Take Care Marketing (IT product reseller), Svenska Lek (Swedish Toys), Agenda 21 (The national adaptation of the UN International Environment Program), UppsalaUniversity, Nocom Nordic Communication, SDR Svensk Direktreklam (Swedish Direct Marketing), Nexus, SVA Statens Veterinärmedicinska Anstalt (National Veterinary Institute of Sweden), Svenska kyrakan (The National Church of Sweden) Sweden Music/Polar Music, Warner/Chappell Music Scandinavia.

Map of the book

			Tasks	Vocabulary	Grammar	Phrasebook
Retail	**1** Departures *page 6*	A	Describe places; Ask for and give information	Features of a location	Question forms (Grammar backup p. 12)	
		B	Give and ask about reasons; Listen to reasons	Compound nouns; Airport shops and purchases		Giving reasons
		C	Understand signs; Understand and give directions; Listen for directions	Airport facilities and airport procedures	Modal verbs (Grammar backup p. 13)	
	2 Purchases *page 14*	A	Listen to a shop transaction; Deal with foreign currency transactions		Question tags (Grammar backup p. 20)	
		B	Find out about layouts and displays; Listen to an interview; Make and respond to suggestions	Locations; Referring words		Making and responding to suggestions
		C	Read and write a postcard; Describe holiday gifts; Listen to a conversation; Express likes and preferences		Numbers and quantities (Grammar backup p. 21)	Likes and preferences
	3 Responsibilities *page 22*	A	Read and write about careers	*Work for / work as*	Past continuous (Grammar backup p. 28)	
		B	Read correspondence; Open formal and informal letters; Write a reply to a fax	Verbs for placing orders		Opening formal responses
		C	Listen to interviews; Talk about skills and qualities; Read about work experience; Give an interview		*Used to* (Grammar backup p. 29)	
	4 At your service *page 30*	A	Interpret signs; Read a newspaper article; Express possibilities and certainties		First conditional sentences (Grammar backup p. 36)	Possibilities and certainties
		B	Listen to conversations and announcements; Take part in service transactions; Make requests; Ask for a description			Making requests
		C	Read a newspaper article; Change money; Listen to a conversation at an exchange desk	Currencies and financial words		
Manufacturing	**5** On show *page 38*	A	Talk about exhibitions; Listen to an interview; Write a follow-up letter	Exhibitions	Revision of tenses (Grammar backup p. 44)	
		B	Read about a company; Listen to a conversation; Describe personal responses	Business activities; Emphasising adverbs; Responses to food		Describing responses
		C	Talk about specifications; Read promotional signs; Listen to a conversation; Make a sale		Comparisons and degrees of difference (Grammar backup p. 45)	Degrees of difference
	6 On the market *page 46*	A	Read an introduction to a company	Compound words	Defining relative clauses (Grammar backup p. 52)	
		B	Listen to a description of a product range; Describe objects and products; Listen to an interview	Containers; Shapes		
		C	Talk about market research; Interpret data; Explain changes	Fast food outlets; Verbs used to describe changes		Interpreting data
	7 In production *page 54*	A	Read about production processes; Listen to a description of a production process; Describe a production process		Present perfect passive (Grammar backup p. 60)	
		B	Listen to and describe qualities for a job	Factory jobs; Personal qualities and skills	Adverbs (Grammar backup p. 61)	
		C	Discuss job responsibilities; Read about a job; Listen to a description of a product sheet; Read and write faxes and accompanying letters	Phrases of purpose, reason and result		
	8 Exporting *page 62*	A	Listen to an interview; Describe tasks; Listen to a job description; Describe continuing change; Write a fax	Exporting	*Have* something *done* (Grammar backup p. 68)	Describing continuing change
		B	Read about franchises; Make hypothetical statements	Franchise businesses; Nouns ending in *-ee/-er*	2nd conditional sentences (Grammar backup p. 69)	
		C	Describe a receptionist's duties; Receive a visitor; Understand and take messages; Say no politely	Reception duties		Receiving a visitor

Sound Checks: Word stress *page 37*; Sounds and spelling *page 53*; Running words together *page 77*; Intonation *page 125*

			Tasks	Vocabulary	Grammar	Phrasebook
Media	**9** On screen page 70	A	Read the results of a survey; Discuss programme types; Understand and describe preferences; Read and write a viewer profile	Programme types; Compounds with *well-* and *badly-*		Describing preferences
		B	Talk and read about a company; Listen for main points; Rephrasing; Read and write slogans			Rephrasing
		C	Talk about events; Read and write a letter	Reporting verbs	Reported speech *(Grammar backup p. 76)*	
	10 Market research page 78	A	Read about market research; Write questions; Carry out market research	Phrasal verbs	Phrasal verbs *(Grammar backup p. 84)*	
		B	Discuss ways of getting feedback; Read a press release; Talk about information in a table; Read and write about the results of a survey; Compare and contrast	Marketing words		Comparing and contrasting
		C	Talk about viewing figures; Listen to an interview; Interpret a chart; Summarise information from a chart	Audience research; Collective nouns	So / neither / nor *(Grammar backup p. 85)*	
	11 At work page 86	A	Read and talk about conditions of employment; Listen to an interview; Interview someone and report your findings	Working lives	Passive structures with *get* *(Grammar backup p. 92)*	
		B	Read an article; Interview someone; Read and write a CV and a letter of application		Present perfect continuous *(Grammar backup p. 93)*	
		C	Read a job advertisement; Talk about interviews; Listen to an extract from a talk on interview techniques; Listen to an extract from a job interview; Interview someone; Present yourself	Personal qualities		Presenting yourself
	12 In the news page 94	A	Talk about presenting news; Listen to an interview; Read about a person's career path; Talk about work experience		Past perfect *(Grammar backup p. 100)*	
		B	Talk about foreign language use; Read an interview extract; Read information from a news agency; Write and present a news report		Extended noun phrases *(Grammar backup p. 101)*	
		C	Talk about reasons for writing; Recognise types of mistake; Improve a letter and fax; Write a fax from notes			
Services	**13** On line page 102	A	Read an introduction to a company; Compare marketing methods		Linking words *(Grammar backup p. 108)*	
		B	Talk about the Internet; Read Web site pages; Listen to a talk on Web site design; Read and write messages	Computer commands		
		C	Read and talk about fear of technology; Talk about things you do and do not regret		Third conditional sentences *(Grammar backup p. 109)*	Regrets and no regrets
	14 Our environment page 110	A	Discuss environmental problems; Listen to an interview; Listen and take notes; Write from notes; Make recommendations	Resources		
		B	Read and write minutes; Listen to meetings; Make recommendations		Future perfect *(Grammar backup p. 116)*	Making recommendations
		C	Talk about waste disposal; Read about a local campaign; Discuss proposals	Projects	*-ing* forms *(Grammar backup p. 117)*	Accepting and rejecting proposals
	15 The information age page 118	A	Listen to an interview; Read a newspaper report; Talk about information overload	Suffixes	Articles – *a / an*, *the*, no article *(Grammar backup p. 124)*	
		B	Read and prioritise correspondence; Write responses	Collocations		
		C	Talk about electronic mail; Read and write e-mail messages; End e-mail messages			Endings in e-mail messages
	16 Under pressure page 126	A	Talk about secretarial tasks and qualities; Read a survey extract; Listen to a secretary; Discuss doing personal tasks	Secretarial tasks and qualities		
		B	Talk about dealing with customer services; Listen to a staff trainer; Listen to a difficult customer; Discuss personal experiences	Qualities and attitudes	*Should have (done)* *(Grammar backup p. 132)*	
		C	Talk and read about complaints; Listen to a complaint and complete a form; Make and deal with a complaint		*Can't have / must have / might have (done)* *(Grammar backup p. 133)*	Handling a complaint

Learning Skills *page 134*   Tapescripts *page 138*

Retail Departures

1

Action A

- Describe places
- Ask for and give information
- Vocabulary:
    features of a location
- Grammar:
    question forms

Background

Speaking and Reading: describing places

1 Work in pairs. Think about the main features of towns and cities.

a List words and phrases under these headings.

Geography	Climate	People	Business activities
north	wet	warm	tourist industry
hills	windy	population	fishing

b Discuss the features of the town that you are living in. Make notes on information that will interest visitors.

c What do you think tourists dislike about your town?

2 Look at the photographs (1 – 3) and the texts (A – C) below.

a What do the photographs show?
b Read the texts quickly. Match each text with a photograph.
c Read the first text again. How is Alicante different from your own town?

A The city of Alicante lies between the mountains and the sea on the east coast of Spain. It has a population of 260,000 and most of its income is from the tourist industry. Alicante has all the facilities of a city – shops, bars, restaurants and parks – but most tourists come for the beautiful beaches and the wonderful climate. The average temperature is 18ºC and there are 302 sunny days each year.

B Alicante airport is 10 kilometres from the city centre. Four million people use the airport each year – tourists and an increasing number of business people.

C Isabel and Andrew are the manager and deputy manager of W H Smith, one of the airport shops. Isabel is from Barcelona, in Spain, and Andrew is British. They were both in Britain in the early 1990s but they moved to Alicante and opened the shop in 1995.

Speaking and Writing: asking for information

3 Work in pairs.

a Make a question for each answer below, with reference to all three texts. Use one of these question words:

| When? | How many? | Why? | Who? |
| Where? | What? | | |

- On the east coast of Spain.
- 260,000.
- Because they like the beaches and the climate.
- 302.
- 18° Centigrade.
- 4,000,000 a year.
- Tourists and business people.
- The manager and deputy manager of WH Smith.
- From Barcelona.
- In Britain.
- In 1995.

b Now write the questions down.

Grammar: question forms

4 Look at your questions from Exercise 3.

a Which verb forms follow the question words in your questions? What other verb forms can follow question words? Make a list.

When	did	
How many (people)	.....	
Why	.....	
Who	.....	..... ?
Where	.....	
What	.....	

b How are the forms of the questions below different from each other? Why are they different?
- How many people live in Alicante?
- Where does Isabel come from?

c Write questions about the texts on page 6 for these answers. This time, do not use question words.
- No, it isn't.   *Is Alicante in Portugal?*
- Yes, it has.
- Yes, they do.
- Yes, she is.
- No, he wasn't.
- No, it didn't.

p.12 **Grammar backup 1**

Talking point

WORKING IN AN AIRPORT SHOP HAS ITS OWN SPECIAL PROBLEMS.

What do *you* think?

5 Write ten questions that you would like to ask Isabel and Andrew about themselves and about the shop. Keep your questions until you reach the end of Unit 4. Write the answers when you are given the information.

Writing: giving information

6 Work in pairs. Prepare a written text for a tourist brochure about the town that you are living in. Compare it with the texts of other students. Can you improve yours?

Retail

Action B

- Give and ask about reasons
- Listen to reasons
- Vocabulary:
  compound nouns
  airport shops and purchases

W H Smith

Speaking: airport shops and purchases

1 **Discuss these questions.**

a What do people want to buy at airports? Make a list.

b So what kinds of shops do they need? Match the products on your list to types of shops.

    EXAMPLE: *shampoo – chemist's*

2 **Look at the photograph of W H Smith, in Alicante airport. What can you see on the shelves? What other things do you think the shop sells?**

Reading: background information

3 **Read the text below and then work in pairs.**

a Complete the text with suitable verbs.

> The first W H Smith [1]..... in London in 1792. For many years the firm [2]..... known for its station bookshops – at one time there [3]..... over 1,000. Slowly, though, the shops [4]..... into town and city centres. There [5]..... now more than 400 high street shops, and 76 railway and airport shops. The W H Smith Group also [6]..... a chain of shops called Virgin Our Price, which sells music, videos and computer games, and Waterstone's bookshops. It [7]..... 30,000 people.

b Why do you think railway stations and airports are important locations for W H Smith?

8

Unit **1B**

Vocabulary: compound nouns

4 Look at the text on page 8 again.

a Find compound nouns that mean:
- bookshops in railway stations
- shops in high streets
- shops in airports
- games for computers
- centres of cities

b What do you think these compounds mean? Ask and answer.

EXAMPLE: A: *What are bookshelves?*
                      B: *They're shelves for books.*

- bookshelves
- street market
- traveller's cheque
- address book
- cash machine
- newspaper stand
- telephone card

c Make other compounds from the two parts of *telephone card*.
- telephone .....
- ..... card

Listening and Speaking: giving reasons

5 W H Smith already has airport shops in Britain and the United States. Listen to Carmen, who works as a sales assistant at the airport shop in Alicante. Then discuss these questions. Add your own ideas.

a Why did W H Smith choose Alicante for its first airport shop on the continent of Europe?
b Why do travellers come into the shop?
c What special skills do the assistants there need?

6 Listen again.

a Complete these sentences.
- They come in ..... a newspaper or magazine for the plane.
- Some people are impatient or rude ..... they're in a hurry.
- Other people have a lot of time before they catch their plane, ... they stop and chat.
- Then some people come ..... help.

b Write questions for the answers in a above.

c Now complete these sentences so they mean the same as the sentences in a.
- They come in because ..... .
- Some people are in a hurry, so ..... .
- Other people stop for ....., because ..... .
- Then some people come because ..... .

7 Look back at your list of purchases from Exercise 1. Ask and answer about people's reasons for buying particular products:

a when they arrive at an airport.
b before they catch a plane.

Use expressions from the *Phrasebook* to help you.

Phrasebook

Giving reasons

Why do people buy a newspaper before they catch a plane?
For the plane journey.
Because they want to read news of their own country.
To pass the time.
So they can do the crossword.

---

8 Work in pairs. Imagine that you have a product to sell.

a What is your product?
b Who do you expect to buy it?
c What are the advantages and disadvantages of selling products in each of the places below? Which places are best for your product? Why?
- In airport shops.
- In high street shops.
- In street markets.
- At railway stations.
- In local shops.
- Through mail order catalogues.
- In other places.

Report your decisions to the class.

Retail

Action C

- Understand signs
- Understand and give directions
- Listen for directions
- Vocabulary:
  airport facilities and airport procedures
- Grammar:
  modal verbs

Taking off

Speaking: understanding signs

1 Look at the airport signs and the list of airport facilities.

a What does each sign show?

b Which signs are not on the list of facilities?

c On which floor is:
  - the departure area?
  - W H Smith?
  - the arrivals hall?
  - the car hire office?

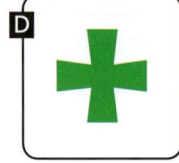

Airport facilities

GROUND FLOOR
Arrivals
Car hire
Chemist's
Police
Tourist office

FIRST FLOOR
Airline offices
Airport information
Coffee shop
Exchange bureau
Lost and found
Ticket sales

SECOND FLOOR
Departures
  In the departure lounge:
  - Airport information
  - Bar
  - Burger King
  - Duty-free shop
  - Exchange
  - Häagen-Dazs ice-cream
  - Restaurant
  - The Tie Gallery
  - Virgin Electronics

  Outside the departure lounge:
  - Coffee shop
  - W H Smith

Listening: directions

2 🎧 Listen to two conversations between staff of W H Smith and travellers.

a Note down what each person wants and where they need to go.

b Listen again. Complete the conversations.

Traveller: Can you ....., please? I must ..... my pesetas back into pounds before I leave.

Raquel: Yes, well the exchange bureau is ....., but it's ..... departure lounge. I'm afraid you can't ..... money until you go through the security check.

Traveller: Oh, right. Thank you.

Traveller: Excuse me. I left my bag ..... somewhere and now I can't ..... it.

Nuria: You needn't ..... . The security guards have probably taken it. You should ..... at the Lost and Found office. It's ....., on the ground floor. You can ..... the stairs, just ....., or the escalators.

Traveller: Oh, thanks a lot.

10

Grammar: modal verbs

3 Look back at the conversations in Exercise 2. Find verbs that are followed by other verbs.

a Which form of the verb follows them?

b Consider the functions that *can*, *must* and *should* help to express. Which of the sentences below expresses:
  • obligation? • advice? • possibility?

You can
You must | change your foreign currency before you leave the country.
You should

c What meaning is *can* used to express in each of these sentences?
  • Of course I can ride a bicycle!
  • You can go if you want to, but don't be late home.

d Use the sentences on the right to explain the uses of modal verbs in the sentences on the left.

You shouldn't
You mustn't | leave your luggage here. | It is not permitted.
You can't   It is not necessary.
You needn't   It is not a good idea.

 p.13 **Grammar backup 1**

Vocabulary: airport procedures

4 Imagine that a young friend is flying alone for the first time. Give him some advice by putting these procedures and suggestions in a sensible order. Use a dictionary to help you.

have a drink	get your boarding card
go through security checks	watch the departures board
wait in the departure lounge	phone me
board the plane	arrive early
check in	

Now explain the procedures to your friend in your own words. Add advice about procedures that are *not* necessary, permitted or a good idea.

EXAMPLE: *You must arrive early, because there are sometimes queues at the check-in desks. You needn't arrive more than two hours before, though, because the desks aren't open.*

Speaking: directions

5 Work in pairs. Imagine that you are at W H Smith.

A: You work in the shop. Look at the list of facilities on page 10 and give help.

B: You are a traveller and you have the following problems. Ask for help:

a You left your bag outside the shop, and now it has gone.

b You are looking for something to eat.

Then change roles.

A: Your problems are:

a You need to buy some gifts quickly before your flight is called.

b You have arrived late to meet a friend from Britain. You can't find him.

Word file Unit 1

SHOPS
airport shop *n*
chain *n*
chemist's *n*
deputy manager *n*
duty-free shop *n*
firm *n*
high street shop *n*
local shop *adj + n*
mail order *n*
catalogue *n*
manager *n*
newspaper stand *n*
queue *n*
station bookshop *n*
street market *n*

AIRPORTS
airline office *n*
arrivals board *n*
boarding card *n*
business people *n pl*
car hire *n*
car park *n*
cash machine *n*
charter flight *n*
check in *v* (check-in *adj/n*)
departure lounge *n*
departures *n*

departures board *n*
escalator *n*
exchange bureau *n*
meeting point *n*
security check *n*
tourist *n*
tourist office *n*
traveller's cheque *n*

PEOPLE
impatient *adj*
population *n*
rude *adj*
warm *adj*

BUSINESS ACTIVITIES
fishing *n*
income *n*
industry *n*
tourist industry *n*

GEOGRAPHY
beach *n*
climate *n*
hill *n*
mountain *n*
sea *n*
wet *adj*
windy *adj*

Grammar backup 1

Question forms

Practice

1 Complete the questions with the correct question word.

a *Where* do you live? Near the station, in the High Street.
b ..... did you see when you went to the meeting? Peter James.
c ..... do you usually do in the evening? Have dinner and watch TV.
d ..... are you going to phone him? Because I haven't got the sales figures for this quarter.
e ..... people were there at the party? Over a hundred.
f ..... can you buy envelopes near here? At W H Smith.
g ..... will I see you next? At the meeting on Tuesday.

2 Write questions for the answers.

a He's an engineer.
  What does he do?
b Yesterday? I went to a conference.
c They're going next week.
d We met him at the station.
e Sandra faxed it.
f I can speak two languages, French and Spanish.
g Because I need English to get a better job.

3 Correct the mistakes.

a Does she ~~to~~ speak Italian? Yes, she does.
  Does she speak Italian? Yes, she does.
b When he is going to write to them? Tomorrow.
c How many meetings has got she next week? Six!
d Who is your name? Thomas Kelly.
e Do you like your job? Yes, I like.
f Do you have got much work to do today? Yes, I'm very busy.
g Will you speak to her later? Yes, I'll.

4 Translation

Write these sentences in your own language. Then close your Course Book. Translate the sentences back into English.

a Did you go on holiday last year? Yes, I did.
b Who do you want to see?
c Who wants to see you?
d Are you studying English at the moment? Yes, I am.

Reference

How many	have you	got?	Two.
Why	are you	learning English?	To get a better job.
Where	do you	live?	In London.
What	did you	do last night?	I watched TV.
	Does he	speak French?	Yes, he does.
	Have you	been to Alicante?	No, I haven't.

- Auxiliary verbs usually come before the subject of a question: What **has he** got in his suitcase? When **did the police** arrive?
- We use the full form of the auxiliary in positive short answers: Have you been to Alicante? Yes, I **have**.
- With the verb *to be* and modal verbs, we do not use another auxiliary verb: **Were you** at home last night? **Can you** phone back?
- *Who*, *what* and *how many* can be the subject of a question. We do not use *do / does / did* when the question word is a subject: **Who visits** Alicante airport? **How many people live** in Alicante?

12

Modal verbs

Practice

1 **Complete the sentences with *must*, *mustn't*, *can*, *can't*, *should*, *shouldn't* or *needn't*.**

a I'd like a hot drink. *Can* I have a cup of tea, please?
b I don't feel very well. Do you think I ..... go to the doctor?
c I'm sorry, I ..... speak to you now because I'm in a hurry. What about tomorrow?
d How many languages ..... you speak?
 Three, including English.
e Why ..... I drive without a seat belt?
 Because it's illegal!
f You ..... take your car to the conference because I'm taking mine. You can come with me.
g In England, you ..... drive on the left of the road.
h You look tired. You ..... go to bed late all the time.

2 **Correct the sentences.**

       needn't
a She ~~needs not~~ ask me – she already knows the answer!
b He must to go to Germany tomorrow for a meeting.
c He doesn't must tell her. It's a secret.
d Cans he speak Spanish fluently?
e When do we should leave this evening?

3 **Translation**

Write these sentences in your own language. Then close your Course Book. Translate the sentences back into English.

a Can you speak English? Yes, I can.
b Do you have to go to work every day? No, I don't.
c You needn't be here until 8 o'clock.
d They mustn't leave too late.
e She should go to the doctor.

Reference

- We use *must*, *mustn't*, *can*, *can't*, *should*, *shouldn't* and *needn't* to express different functions.

Obligation	You **must** be at work by 9 o'clock. They **mustn't** be rude to their customers.
Possibility	You **can** change money in the departure lounge.
Permission	You **can** leave now. You **can't** leave your bag here.
Advice	You **should** ask at the airline office. She **shouldn't** work so hard.
Necessity	She **needn't** check in her hand luggage.
Ability	We **can** help you. I **can't** find my ticket.

- *Must*, *can* and *should* are followed by an infinitive without *to*. There is no *s* with *he* or *she*: **Can** you **help** me? She **must go** through a security check.
- We do not use an auxiliary to form questions with *must*, *can* and *should*: **Should I** buy some traveller's cheques?
- The positive form of *needn't* is *need to*. *Need to* is a full verb, not a modal. It also has a negative form, *don't need to* (an alternative form to *needn't*) and a question form: **Do you need to** leave already?
- We often use *have to* instead of *must* in questions: **Do** I **have to** check in over there?
- *Can't* is common in spoken English. *Cannot* is used in formal writing.

Retail Purchases

2

Action A

- Listen to a shop transaction
- Deal with foreign currency transactions
- Grammar: question tags

On the till

Speaking and Listening: a shop transaction

1   Look at the photographs.
a   Find these:

> the customer   the sales assistant   the counter   a bag
> the till   a badge   a poster   batteries   a magazine

b   Answer these questions.
- Does the shop accept credit cards?
- How is the customer paying?
- Is he Spanish, do you think?
- What do you think his hobby is?
- Where are the plastic bags kept?

c   Put the pictures in order. Is there more than one possible order?

2   Now listen to a conversation between Nuria and a customer.
a   Did you put the pictures in the correct order?
b   How much money did the customer give Nuria?
c   How much change did she give him?

3   Which of these expressions did Nuria or the customer use? They are all possible. Listen again and check.
a   Can I have this magazine, please? / I'd like this magazine, please.
b   Are you paying in pounds? / How would you like to pay?
c   How much is it? / This one's 600 pesetas, isn't it?
d   Here you are. / There you are.
e   Your change. / Here's your change.
f   Do you want a bag? / Would you like a bag?

14

Unit 2A

Grammar: question tags

4  Look at these sentences from Exercise 3.

How much is it? Are you paying in pounds?

a Listen and repeat the questions. Does the speaker's voice rise or fall at the end of each?

b Now listen to two different ways of asking the following question. What is the difference?
This one's 600 pesetas, isn't it?

c How is the question in b formed?

d Look at other questions. How are these questions formed? Can you make general rules?
- I've seen you before, *haven't I?*
- Your mother bought some magazines last week, *didn't she?*
- You often come here, *don't you?*

5 Practise using question tags.

a Make these statements into questions by adding question tags.
- You're Andrew.
- A plane has just arrived from Britain.
- We've got some new magazines.
- I can go now.
- She enjoys her work.
- We took more money yesterday.

b Work in pairs. Check information about your partner.
EXAMPLES: *You're in the accounts department, aren't you?*
You work part-time, don't you?

▶ p.20 **Grammar backup 2**

Listening and Speaking: foreign currency transactions

6  Look at the conversation. What do you think the customer says? Listen and check.

Nuria: Hello. Can I help you?
Customer: Yes, I'd like this book, please, but ..... .
Nuria: That's all right. We take pounds. What does the price tag say?
Customer: .....
Nuria: One thousand one hundred. That's five pounds, please.

7 Sales assistants at W H Smith use conversion charts for British pounds and American dollars.

a How many pesetas were there to one pound on this particular day?

b How much are the objects above in pounds?

c Work in pairs.

A: Take the part of Nuria. Serve your customer. There are one hundred pence to a British pound.

B: You are a customer. Buy one or more of the things in the pictures. Pay in pounds.

770 ptas.
1,980 ptas.
1,320 ptas.
220 ptas.

POUNDS	PESETAS
£1	220
£5	1,100
£10	2,200
£15	3,300
£20	4,400
£25	5,500
£30	6,600
£35	7,700
£40	8,800
£45	9,900
£50	11,000
£75	16,500
£100	22,000

Retail

Action B — On display

- Find out about layouts and displays
- Listen to an interview
- Make and respond to suggestions
- Vocabulary:
  locations
  referring words

Speaking and Reading: shop layouts

1 Discuss these questions.

a It is said that the position of products in shops affects what we buy. Do you think this is true? Give examples.

b Look at the plan of W H Smith in Alicante. Where do you expect to find:
   • newspapers?   • sweets?   • cigarettes?

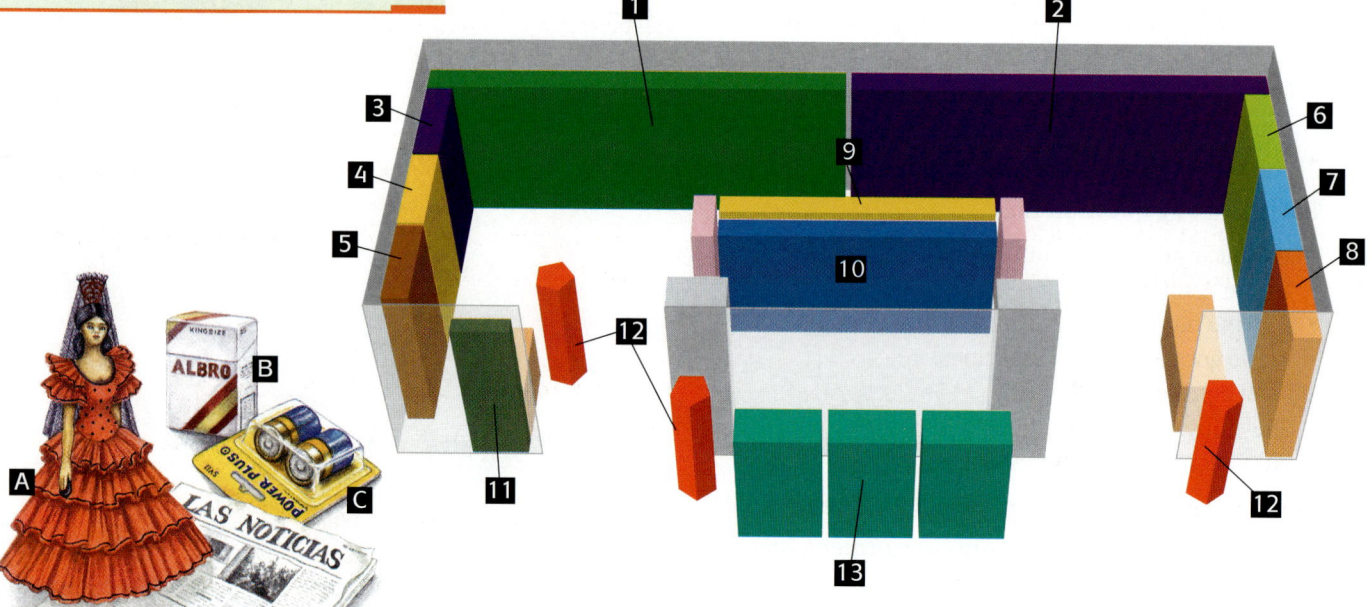

2 Read about W H Smith. Andrew, the deputy manager, is describing the layout of the shop and particular displays. Match the products above with their position in the shop. Which items are not shown in the pictures?

'The shop, as you can see on this plan, is long and narrow. The newspaper stands are on display in front of the shop – so you can pick up a paper and then come in and pay. You can also choose postcards out there, though there's another stand inside, near one of the counters. As you come in, books and magazines are facing you on the far wall, and there are more books on the ends of the central display unit. Sweets and chocolate bars are displayed on the near side of that unit, here. The idea is that you can see them from outside through the glass windows. Souvenirs and presents, like typical Spanish sweets and dolls, are on the far side, facing the back wall. We keep cigarettes here, behind the left-hand counter, and things like batteries behind the other counter. Then in the far left-hand corner of the shop are the Disney products – toys and stationery. On the same shelves, but towards the front of the shop, we have children's books and then maps and guidebooks. On the other end wall, ordinary stationery items like diaries and notebooks are at the back, and closer to the counter are travel accessories and games.'

Talking point

What do *you* think?

Vocabulary: locations and referring words

3   Read the text again. Find words and expressions that contain the opposites of the words in bold.

a   **a long way from** one of the counters
b   on the **near** wall
c   facing the **front** wall
d   the **right-hand** counter
e   towards the **back** of the shop
f   **further from** the counter

4   Explain what these words and phrases in *italics* refer to.

a   *you* (line 1, line 2)   Who?
b   *then* (line 3)   When?
c   *out there* (line 4)   Where?
d   *that unit* (line 8)   Which unit?
e   *the other counter* (line 12)   Which other counter?
f   *the same shelves*   Which shelves?
    (lines 13 – 14)
g   *the other end wall* (line 15)   Which wall?

Listening to an interview

5   You are going to hear Andrew talking about the layout of the shop. Discuss these questions. Then listen and check.

a   When and why does the display of books and magazines change?
b   How are sweets displayed? What is the effect of this display?
c   How are children persuaded to look at children's books?
d   Andrew describes tobacco as an 'impulse purchase'. What do you think that means?
e   Where is the chewing gum? Why?
f   What does Andrew say are 'high-risk items'? What does he mean?

Listening and Speaking: making suggestions

6   Look at the photograph. What are Isabel and Carmen doing? What do you think they are talking about?

7   Listen to two people discussing the display of goods in another shop.

a   What kind of shop is it?
b   What is the problem?
c   What are the possible solutions?

8   Listen again. Complete these suggestions.

a   Shall we .....?
b   I suppose we could ..... .
c   Let's ..... .
d   And why don't we .....?
e   Oh, and have you thought about .....?

Which form of the verb follows each expression?

Phrasebook

Making and responding to suggestions

We could change the display.
I suppose we could add something.
Why don't we buy some new stock?
How about putting up some new signs?
Have you thought about moving them?
Let's replace these magazines.
Shall we advertise more?
Good idea.
Yes, or we could send them back.
Yes, let's do that.
No, I don't think it will work.

---

9   Work in pairs. Look at the room you are in. Imagine that you are opening a branch of W H Smith. Discuss where to put a counter and the products. Use the *Phrasebook* to help you.

Retail

| Action | C |

On holiday

■ Read and write a postcard
■ Describe holiday gifts
■ Listen to a conversation
■ Express likes and preferences
■ Grammar:
   numbers and quantities

Reading: a holiday postcard

1 Look at the postcard below.

a Which paragraph is about:
   • daily life on holiday?   • Sue's general opinion of the holiday?
   • a future plan?

b Where can you add these sentences to make a longer postcard?
   • It's not very far on the train.
   • It's crowded but beautiful, and the sea is warm.
   • I'm looking forward to seeing you all.
   • What a change from Birmingham!
   • I want to buy some presents before we leave.

c What features of the language of the postcard are informal?

July 7th

Dear Everyone

We're having a great time in Benidorm and it's wonderful to be away from the office.

The weather's fantastic, and we're spending most of our time on the beach. At midday, when it's really hot, we have a slow lunch and then go back to the hotel for a short siesta. All this sunbathing makes us so tired!

Tomorrow Dave and I are going to Alicante to do some shopping. I hope you're not working too hard!

Love, Sue

Accounts Dept.
Parktown Ltd.
Bell Street
Birmingham RG1 6MT

Speaking: holiday gifts

2 **The photograph on the right shows a traditional British seaside sweet called rock, which is sold by W H Smith, Alicante.**

a Discuss gifts that you have received from people returning from holiday. Which ones have you used? Which did you not like? Why?

b Imagine that you are opening a gift shop in a holiday town in your country. What local products do you think holidaymakers will want to buy? Agree with other people in the class what you will stock.

18

Listening to a conversation

3 🎧 **Listen to two people discussing the local Spanish products opposite.**

a Which gifts will they buy, do you think?

b Which ones do they describe as:

cheap	beautiful	fun	tasteful
quite nice	expensive	not very attractive
boring	tasteless	awful	lovely

c Add other adjectives to the list above.

Grammar: numbers and quantities

4 🎧 **Listen to the conversation again.**

a What do the words in bold refer to?
Would Jane like **one of those**?
I don't think she'd like **either of them** much.
None of them. They're all awful.
She doesn't really need **any of these things**.

b Do these expressions refer to a choice of two things, or more than two?

either of them	all of them
none of them	neither of them
(not) any of them	both of them
one of them	some of them

c Which phrases below mean the same as *none*? Which means the same as *neither*? Use a dictionary to help you.
• not one • not either • not any

d Work in pairs. Which of these sentences is correct? Why are the others not good English?
• We don't want none of those postcards.
• I like both of these dolls; I'd be happy with either of them.
• Neither of them isn't very attractive.

▶▶ p.21 **Grammar backup 2**

Phrasebook

Likes and preferences

I'd like the pot.
My sister would prefer the lace.
We'd love a basket.
John would be happy with the wine.
Tina would rather have the donkey.

Speaking: likes and preferences

5 Work in pairs. Discuss with your partner which of the gifts below you would like to receive. Use adjectives from Exercise 3 and expressions from the *Phrasebook* to help you.

mug, basket, wine, turron, pot, sandals, doll, tablecloth, donkey

Writing a postcard

6 Write a postcard to your English class from a holiday town. Use the same structure as the postcard in Exercise 1: general introduction; everyday activities; future plans; closing words. Do not mention the name of the place. Can other people guess where you are?

Word file Unit 2

SHOPS
counter *n*
dis**play** *n*
dis**play** unit *n*
impulse **pur**chase *n*
layout *n*
seasonal *adj*
stand *n*
till *n*
trans**ac**tion *n*

MONEY
change *n*
con**ver**sion chart *n*
foreign **cur**rency *n*

LOCATION
a **long way** from *prep*
back *n*
close to *prep*

far *adj*
front *n*
left-hand *adj*
near *prep*
right-hand *adj*

NUMBERS
both *pron*
either *pron*
neither *pron*
none *pron*

SOUVENIRS
awful *adj*
basket *n*
boring *adj*
doll *n*
donkey *n*
fun *adj*
mug *n*

quite nice *adv* + *adj*
sandals *n pl*
sweets *n pl*
tablecloth *n*
tasteful *adj*
tasteless *adj*
wine *n*

OTHER WORDS
badge *n*
battery *n*
chewing gum *n*
chocolate bar *n*
ciga**rette** *n*
gift *n*
guidebook *n*
poster *n*
to**bac**co *n*
travel accessory *n*

Grammar *backup 2*

Question tags

Practice

1 Add the question tags.

a She's from Spain, isn't she?
b I'm meeting him at 9.30, ... ?
c A message hasn't arrived for me, ... ?
d She can come tomorrow, ... ?
e There weren't many tills, ... ?
f The reports haven't been sent, ... ?
g They need a battery, ... ?
h I haven't got my change, ... ?
i He likes his job, ... ?
j You wrote to them yesterday, ... ?

2 Correct the mistakes.

a We can't ask them again, ~~do~~ *can* we?
b Does he need to arrive early, doesn't he?
c She's never rude, isn't she?
d There are two faxes on your desk, aren't they?
e She doesn't have to wear a uniform, has she?
f We can't see the manager, can't we?

3 Translation

Write these sentences in your own language. Then close your Course Book. Translate the sentences back into English.

a You want to see him, don't you? Yes, that's right.
b He isn't free today, is he? No, I'm afraid not.
c There aren't many people here today, are there?

Reference

- Tag questions are formed with a statement and a tag. We usually use a negative tag with a positive statement and a positive tag with a negative statement: *He **was** at work yesterday, **wasn't he**? **We don't need** any more information, **do we**?*

- We often use a tag with falling intonation to check something that we believe is true. We often use a tag with rising intonation to check something that we are not sure about: *The plane has arrived, **hasn't it**?* (You believe it has arrived.) *The plane has arrived, **hasn't it**?* (You don't know if it has arrived.)

- We never use a tag after a question.

- If a verb usually has an auxiliary in its question form, an auxiliary is used in the question tag: *Did he **come** late? He **came** late, **didn't** he?*

- The tag for *I am* is *aren't I*: ***I'm** late, **aren't I**?*

- We usually replace the noun in the statement with a pronoun in the tag: ***The company** is doing very well, isn't **it**? **The machines** are all new, aren't **they**?*

- *There* is repeated in the tag: *There are a lot of passengers today, **aren't there**?*

20

Grammar backup 2

Numbers and quantities

Practice

1 Choose the best words to complete the sentences.

a They never have *any* / ~~none~~ interesting souvenirs in stock.
b I like most / all of the display units, but not the one in the corner.
c Which guidebook do you want to buy? Either / Neither of them – you decide.
d One / Both of my colleagues is very impatient.
e All / None of the charter flights has arrived.
f She hasn't got any / some appointments tomorrow.

2 Use the best word to complete the sentences.

| one | neither | both | some | any | ~~most~~ |
| all | none | | | | |

a *Most* of the mail order catalogues have arrived – I'm only waiting for the ones from Geneva.
b They've sold ..... the machines but will have some more next week so we can buy one then.
c Are there ..... questions about the figures? No? Then we can discuss the next report.
d I've got ..... questions to ask about their letter.
e ..... of the cash machines are working. We need the engineer to repair all six of them.
f ..... of them can come to the meeting but not both of them.
g I need two pairs of sandals so I'll buy ..... of them.
h Did you send the letters to Kate and Simona? ..... of them have replied and I need their answers soon.

3 Translation

Write these sentences in your own language. Then close your Course Book. Translate the sentences back into English.

a Neither secretary is at work today.
b I've got some letters to write.
c None of them were late yesterday.
d Most people hate queuing.

Reference

How many magazines does she want?

	0	1	2	3	4	5
She doesn't want **any** of them.	✓					
She wants **none** (of them).	✓					
She'd like **one** (of the magazines).		✓				
She'd like **some** of them.			✓	✓	✓	
She'd like **most** of the magazines.					✓	
She'd like **all** of them.						✓

Which book does she want?

	0	1	2
Either of them / **Either** book.		✓	
Neither of them.	✓		
Both of them.			✓

- We often use words like *both*, *some* and *any* to answer questions that begin with *how many* or *which*. They can be used in four main structures: *I need* **both**; *I need* **both books**; *I need* **both of the books**; *I need* **both of them**.

- *Either* and *neither* are only followed by singular nouns. *Both*, *some*, *most*, and *all* are followed by plural nouns and verbs: *You can ask* **either assistant**. **Both shops** *are open*.

- We never use *none* immediately before a noun: **None** of the **people** speak Spanish.

- *Either*, *neither* and *none* + *of* + plural noun can use a singular or plural verb: **None** of the managers **are** / **is** coming to the meeting.

- *Both* and *some* are mostly used in positive sentences. *Either* and *any* are used in positive sentences when you don't mind which one you have: *I like* **both** *of them.* **Either** *of them is fine.*

21

Retail Responsibilities

3

Action A

- Read and write about careers
- Vocabulary:
  work for / work as
- Grammar:
  past continuous

Careers

Reading about careers

1 Read the texts, and write the dates beside each person's career history below.

Isabel Espinosa was born in Barcelona, in Spain. In 1990 she started working for Paperchase in London. Paperchase sells stationery and gifts, and at that time it was owned by W H Smith. She worked as a sales assistant and, from 1991, as deputy manager in a number of the London shops before she became the manager of the Victoria branch in 1992. While she was running the shop, she also attended training courses. Then in 1995 she was offered the job of manager in W H Smith, Alicante, and she moved back to Spain.

Andrew Thomas is British, and he has worked for W H Smith since 1990. At that time he moved from his home town of Middlesbrough to Liverpool to study languages and international relations. While he was studying, he also worked part-time for W H Smith, both in Liverpool and, in the university holidays, in Middlesbrough. After leaving college in 1994, he went on a management training course run by W H Smith. In 1995 he became deputy manager of the new Alicante branch.

Isabel Espinosa

1995	–	present	Manager, W H Smith, Alicante
.....	–	.....	Manager, Paperchase, Victoria, London
			Attended courses in management, health and safety, stock control etc
.....	–	.....	Deputy Manager, Paperchase, Cheapside and Tottenham Court Road, London
.....	–	.....	Sales assistant, Paperchase, Victoria and Cheapside, London

Andrew Thomas

.....	–	.....	Deputy manager, W H Smith, Alicante
.....	–	.....	W H Smith management training course
.....	–	.....	Sales assistant, W H Smith, Liverpool and Middlesbrough (part-time)

Vocabulary: *work for / work as*

2 Look at the first text again.

a Who did Isabel *work for* in 1990? What did she *work as*?
b And from 1991, who did she *work for*? What did she *work as*?
c Talk about yourself, or a friend who is working, in the same way.

Unit **3A**

Grammar: past continuous

3 **Compare these sentences from the first text.**

She worked as a sales assistant ... before she became the manager of the Victoria branch.
While she was running the shop, she also attended training courses.

a Which sentence tells us that two situations happened during the same time period? Which activity covered the whole period? When did the other activity happen?
b What does the other sentence tell us about the times of activities? Which tenses are used here?
c Find a sentence with a past continuous verb (*was / were* + *-ing* verb form) in the text about Andrew.
d Change the pronoun *he* in this sentence to the pronoun *I* and then *they*. Do the verb forms change?

4 **Look at the picture and work in pairs.**

a What was happening at the shop when the new manager arrived?

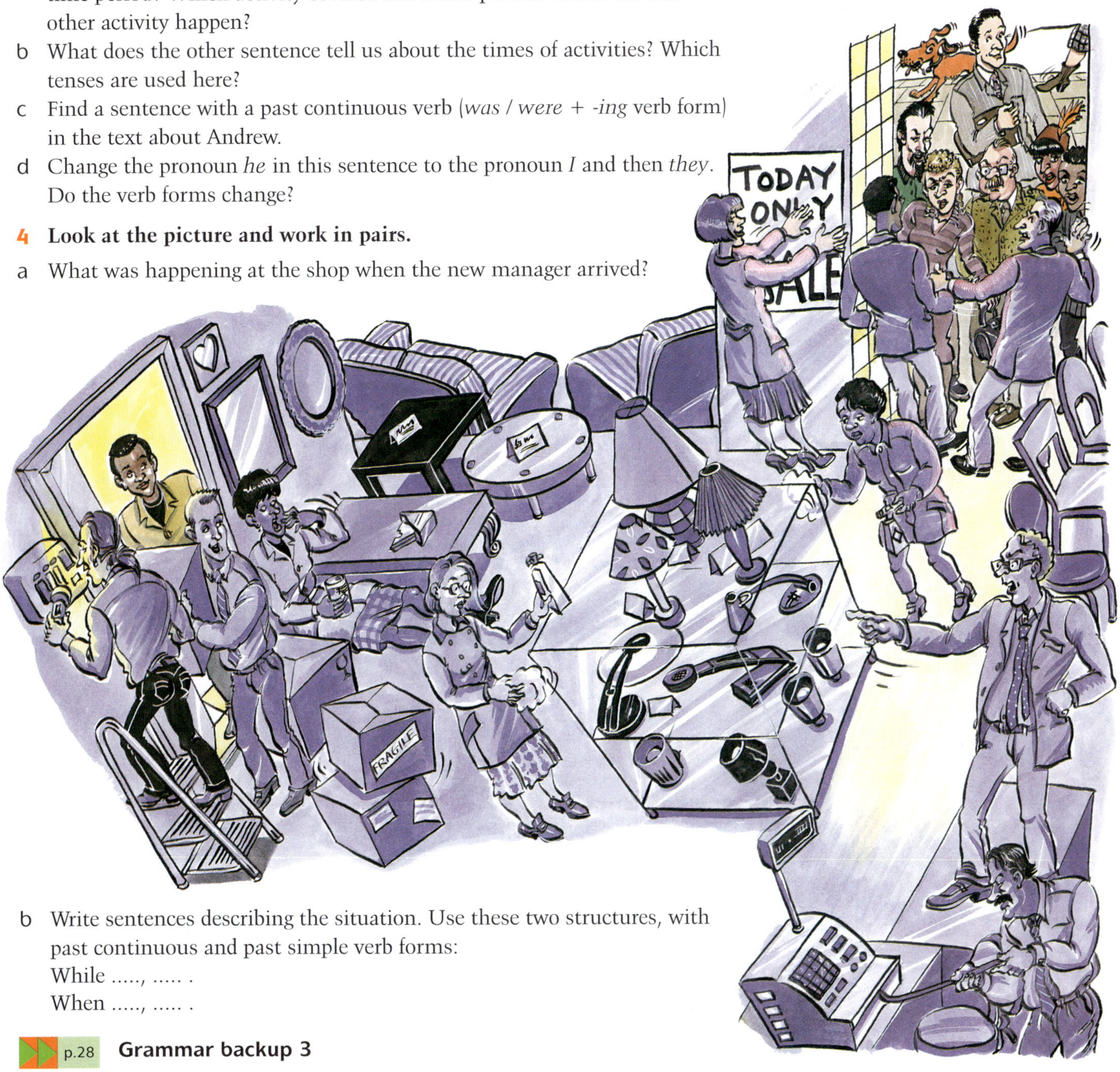

b Write sentences describing the situation. Use these two structures, with past continuous and past simple verb forms:
While ....., ...
When ....., ...

 p.28 Grammar backup 3

Writing a career history

5 **Write about your own career history or the career of a family member.**

a Write notes like those in Exercise 1.
b Write a text like the ones about Isabel and Andrew.

Retail

Action B

- Read correspondence
- Open formal and informal letters
- Write a reply to a fax
- Vocabulary: verbs for placing orders

Paperwork

A

Facsimile transmission

To	WH SMITH		
For the attention of	CLAIRE MACHIN	Facsimile Number	07 44 1793 562651
From	ANDREW THOMAS	Date	11 October 1996
Department	W.H. SMITH ALICANTE	Number of sheets to follow	0 For missing or illegible sheets please call: 00 34 6 69 19264

WH SMITH

W H Smith Limited
Aeropuerto De Alicante
Codigal Postal No: 03071
Alicante
Spain
Telephone 003466919099

Comments

Claire,

Further to our conversation on Wednesday, the books that we would be interested in are for children aged between 6 and 8 (year 2 and year 3). It seems that the school is very interested in sourcing books from us and they have asked if there is a catalogue of titles available. If there is one could you please forward it to me and I will pass it on. With best wishes

Andrew Thomas

B

Facsimile transmission

To	ALICANTE		
For the attention of	ISABEL	Facsimile Number	0034 669 19264
From	KATE HUMPHRIES	Date	5 August 1998
Department	EXPRESS	Number of sheets to follow	0 For missing or illegible sheets please call facsimile operator on extension: 2523

WH SMITH

W H Smith Limited
Greenbridge Road
Swindon SN3 3LD
Telephone (01793) 616161
Facsimile extension 2651

Comments

Dear Isabel

Further to my fax of 2 August, I can now confirm that Brian will visit you on 14/15 August. I have booked him on the following flights:

Date	Flight No	Departs	Arrives
14/8	IB5145	Heathrow 1645	Alicante 2005
15/8	IB5142	Alicante 1430	Heathrow 1555

I understand that you usually arrange for Brian to be met at the airport and book accommodation for him. Please let me know if I can do anything to help.

Many thanks,

Yours sincerely

Kate Humphries

Kate Humphries

SEND TO: W.H. SMITH AIRPORTS DEPOT (ALL ORDERS FOR ALICANTE) NORTHUMBERLAND CLOSE STANWELL STAINES MIDDLESEX TW19 7LN ES133252054	**HarperCollinsPublishers** P.O. Box Glasgow G4 ONB Telephone: Glasgow 0141 722 3200 After Business Hours: 0141 762-0999 Cables: HARPERCOLLINS GLASGOW Telex: 778107 Giro: 105 3159 Facsimile: 0141-306-3119 Order Dept Fax: 0141-762-0584 V.A.T. Reg. No. 259 6397 06	INVOICE TO: W H SMITH + SON LTD (O/SEAS A/C) GREENBRIDGE INDUSTRIAL ESTATE GREENBRIDGE ROAD SWINDON SN3 3LD	**INVOICE** NUMBER 05040900 DATE 30-05-96 PAGE 1 ACCOUNT 261722401 S.A.N. 0000001

INSTRUCTIONS	LOCN :- 000648		ANCA		DESPATCH METHOD	A-06					
PUBLISHER	ISBN	QUANTITY	DESCRIPTION	Recommended Retail Price	CUSTOMER ORDER NUMBER	Pub Day	Date Mth	AGREED PRICE	DISCOUNT PERCENTAGE	NET VALUE	V.A.T. RATE
TRADE	0006482066	30	THANK YOU FOR YOUR ORDER. YOUR CUSTOMER SERVICE CONTACT IS PAUL ON 0141 306 3264 X-FILES VOL 3 - GROUND ZERO	5.99	N. HAYWARD				45.00	98.84	

* Amount due is shown in the Total Section *

TOTAL V.A.T.	TOTAL NET VAL	TOTAL AMOUNT DUE
0.00	98.84	98.84

Unit **3B**

D

```
                    DESPATCH NOTE (R40)
Sent from:   W H Smith Ltd (Branch: 7985)        Page:              1 of 1
Deliver to:  WHS ALICANTE AIRPORT                SAO Number:        SAO35280
Address:     AEROPUERTO DE ALICANTE              Delivery Date:     02/10/96
             CODIGO POSTAL NO. 03071             Packing List No:   035098
             ALICANTE                            Despatch No:       00934851
             SPAIN                               Cust Order No:     ALIC/FILMS/011096
Post Code:              Customer No: 9952
```

Item	Part Number and Description	Ordered	Delivered	Unit Price	Pack Price	Total
0001	KOD015 KODAK GOLD GA135-24 100 (PK5) 3711140	5.00	5.00	3.49	17.45	87.25
0002	KOD016 KODAK GOLD GA135-36 100 (PK5) 372695	5.00	5.00	4.49	22.45	112.25
0003	KOD017 KODAK GOLD GR135-24 200 (PK5) 3714847	5.00	5.00	3.79	18.95	94.75
0004	KOD018 KODAK GOLD GB135-36 200 (PK5) 3724812	5.00	5.00	4.79	23.95	119.75
					Grand Total	414.00

Reading correspondence

1 Look at the different kinds of correspondence.

a Find:
  - faxes.
  - a despatch note.
  - an invoice.

b Which of these:
  - are from W H Smith, Alicante?
  - are being copied to Alicante?
  - are addressed to W H Smith, Alicante?

c Which ones are:
  - a request for payment?
  - a list that arrives with a delivery?
  - a request for a catalogue?
  - for information only?

Vocabulary: verbs for placing orders

2 Find these verbs in the correspondence A – D. Answer the questions and guess the meaning of each verb.

A	*source*	What will the school do after they see the catalogue?
	forward	What should Claire Machin do with the catalogue if she has one?
B	*confirm*	Did Isabel already have a possible date for Brian's visit?
	book	Who will she phone to arrange accommodation for him?
C	*recommend*	What price do the publishers think that *X-Files* should sell for?
D	*despatch*	Where did the Kodak films come from?
	pack	What do you think the films were put into before they left?
	order	Who asked for them?
	deliver	It is October 3rd 1996. Which country are the films in now?

3 Choose verbs from Exercise 2 to complete these sentences.

a I have ..... a seat for him on next Thursday's Iberia flight from Heathrow.
b Could you please ..... those prices in writing?
c Which of your magazines do you ..... for a small shop? We can only take a few titles.
d The books were ..... by lorry last week. They are arriving here tomorrow.
e Is that the sales department? Good. I'd like to ..... some stationery, please.

4 Look at the correspondence again.

a Find the phrase *Further to ...* in the faxes. What follows this phrase in each case? What other expressions can follow it?

b How do the writers end their faxes? Which of the phrases below are more formal? Which are less formal?

Yours sincerely	Many thanks	All the best
With best wishes	Yours	Regards
Yours faithfully	Love	See you soon

Writing a reply to a fax

5 Work in pairs. Choose fax A or B and plan a reply. Decide who is writing, who they are writing to, and what they want to say in the fax. Then write the fax. Include an expression from the *Phrasebook*.

> *Phrasebook*
>
> **Opening formal responses (letters and faxes)**
>
> **Further to** your letter of September 1st, I ...
> **With reference to** our recent telephone conversation, I ...
> **Following** our meeting in Hamburg, I ...

Retail

Action C

- Listen to interviews
- Talk about skills and qualities
- Read about work experience
- Give an interview
- Grammar:
  used to

Sales skills

Speaking and Listening: skills and qualities

1 What kind of person do you think Isabel employs as a sales assistant?

a Make notes on suitable qualities. Then listen and check.
b Work in pairs or small groups. Discuss whether you have the necessary skills and personality to work for Isabel. Which of you is the best person for the job of sales assistant?

Reading about work experience

2 Raquel and Nuria work for Isabel in Alicante. Read about their experience and their hopes for the future.

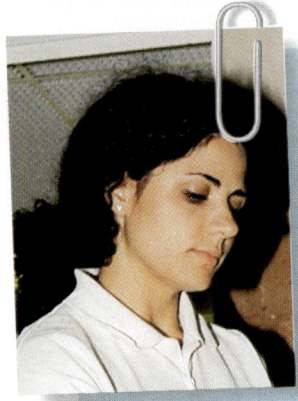

Raquel used to work in another airport shop. Then she did a computing course before joining W H Smith as a sales assistant. She wants to work on planes, though, so she works in the shop from 7 am to 1 pm and between 4.30 pm and 9.30 pm she studies to be a stewardess.

Nuria wants to work in tourism. After she left school, she went to England to learn English. Now she studies tourism in the mornings and English in the afternoons. She works at W H Smith in the evenings. She would like to spend time in Germany, to learn German.

a Make notes about each of them under these headings:
   • Past   • Present   • Future plans
b Why do you think Isabel decided to employ them?

Talking point

What do *you* think?

Unit **3C**

Grammar: *used to*

3 Look at this sentence about Raquel:

Raquel used to work in another airport shop.

a Did she work there regularly, for a period of time?
b Does she work there now?
c What do you think the question and negative forms of *used to* are? Complete these sentences.
 • ..... Raquel ..... study computing? Yes, she did.
 • Nuria ..... study tourism, but she does now.

4 Work in pairs. Think of a time when your life changed dramatically. Explain to your partner what happened and how things were different for you before and after that.

> EXAMPLE: *I moved out of my parents' house three years ago. They used to provide all my meals, but I cook for myself now ...*
>
> *I got my present job last year. I used to be depressed on Monday mornings, but now ...*

 **p.29 Grammar backup 3**

Listening and Speaking: specialist skills

5 Aileen Winter works in a different kind of shop. She runs a florist's in Wales. Work in pairs and discuss these questions.

a Why do people buy flowers?
b What special skills and knowledge do you need to buy and sell them, do you think?
c When do you buy flowers? How do you choose them?

6 Listen and make notes. List the tasks that Aileen does at work.

7 Use a dictionary to help you. Which of these words from her interview refer to:

a flowers?
b business contacts?
c feelings?
d work places?

> wholesaler   storeroom   confident
> workshop   bouquets   displays
> arrangements   distressing   sympathetic

Add two other words to each of the lists.

Speaking: an interview

8 Work in pairs. Choose another type of shop that Aileen might have worked in before she became a florist.

A: Imagine that you are a reporter for a local magazine. Interview Aileen about the differences between her two jobs, and about memorable experiences that she had in each shop.

B: Take the part of Aileen. Answer the reporter's questions.

Word file   Unit 3

TRAINING	shift *n*	QUALITIES
attend *v*	stewardess *n*	confident *adj*
become *v*	wholesaler *n*	flexible *adj*
computing course *n*	work as *v*	personality *n*
	work for *v*	sympathetic *adj*
tourism *n*		
train *v*	CORRESPONDENCE	OTHER WORDS
training course *n*	book *v*	bouquet *n*
	confirm *v*	chat *n*
	despatch *v*	distressing *adj*
JOBS	despatch note *n*	flower arrangement *n*
handle *v*	forward *v*	
own *v*	further to *prep*	identify *v*
run *v*	recommend *v*	storeroom *n*
sales assistant *n*	source *v*	workshop *n*
sales staff *n*		

27

Grammar *backup 3*

Past continuous

Practice

1 Complete the sentences with past continuous or past simple verbs forms.

a I *was leaving* (leave) the office when I *met* (meet) David.
b When I ..... (arrive) in Paris yesterday, it ..... (rain).
c They ..... (not / work) at 7.30 pm last night, they ..... (watch) a football match on TV!
d ..... (she / sleep) when you ..... (phone)? No, she ..... .
e At 7 o'clock last night, Franco and Paul ..... (chat) while Sarah ..... (write) letters.
f They ..... (arrive) for the training course ten minutes early.
g When I ..... (sent) the fax, they ..... (reply) immediately.
h ..... (he / send) the e-mail last night? I think so.

2 Translation

Write these sentences in your own language. Then close your Course Book. Translate the sentences back into English.

a I was still working at 10 o'clock last night.
b They were discussing the latest figures when the managing director arrived.
c Susanna wasn't listening to Paul while he was talking to her.
d Were you at the meeting this morning? No, I was working at home.

Reference

- We use the past continuous to describe a temporary but continuous activity happening at a particular time in the past: *At 11.30, Claire **was serving** a customer in the shop.*

- We also use the past continuous to talk about two or more activities that were happening at the same time in the past. We often use *while* to join the parts of the sentence: *Mark and Louise were talking to Franco **while** Sarah was reading the report.*

- We use the past continuous and the past simple to talk about an action that was already happening when another action happened. We use *when* to join the two parts of the sentence: *They were talking to Franco **when** the phone rang.*

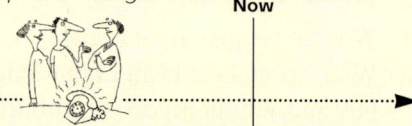

- We also use *when* and the past simple in both clauses to describe two short actions which followed each other: ***When** the customer dropped the mug, it broke.*

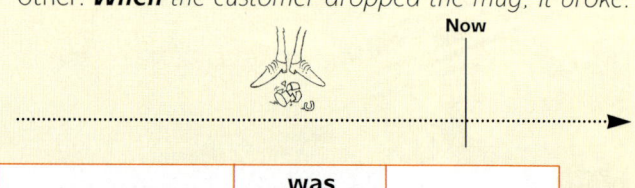

I / he / she / it	was wasn't	working.
You / we / they	were weren't	

Was I / he / she / it	working?
Were you / we / they	

Yes, No,	I / he / she / it	was. wasn't.
Yes, No,	you / we / they	were. weren't.

Used to

Practice

1 Write sentences about what you *used to do* and *didn't use to do* when you were ten years old.

EXAMPLE: *I used to live in Hamburg, but now I live in Cologne.*

2 Correct these sentences.

a Did you ~~used~~ *use* to have your own firm?
b They used drive to work but now they take the train.
c We not use to work shifts but now we do.
d I use to work for an airline office.
e Did she use to work as a deputy manager? Yes, she worked.
f I used to smoke for ten years.

3 Translation

Write these sentences in your own language. Then close your Course Book. Translate the sentences back into English.

a I used to enjoy watching cartoons when I was a child.
b They didn't use to like attending training courses.
c How did you use to travel to work?
d I usually go to the cinema at the weekend.

Reference

- We use *used to* to describe events or situations that happened in the past but do not happen now: *I **used to** share a flat, but now I've got my own house. I **didn't use to** like seafood, but I love it now. **Did** he **use to** play tennis? He doesn't take any exercise these days.*

- *Used to* also refers to a past habit. We use the present simple to talk about present habits: *He **used to** smoke. He **doesn't smoke** now.*

- We use the past simple, not *used to*, to describe how long a situation continued: *I **lived** in Leeds for 3 years.*

I You He She It We They	used to didn't use to	live near here.

	I you he she it we they	use to	live near here?	Yes, I **did**. / No, she **didn't**.
Did				

Retail
At your service

4

Action A

- Interpret signs
- Read a newspaper article
- Express possibilities and certainties
- Grammar: first conditional sentences

Retail strategies

Discussion: interpreting signs

1 Look at the departure board. What should you do if you are flying to:

a Antalya?   b Vienna?   c Toronto?

					11.50
Flight	**Destination**	**Time**	**Boarding**	**Gate**	**Remarks**
SSP 2138	Antalya	12.10	11.50	2	
RIP 672	Vienna	12.20			CANCELLED
PLA 113	Toronto	12.25	16.00		DELAYED

2 How do you think these passengers for Toronto will spend the next few hours?

a a businesswoman flying home from an important meeting
b a family with small children
c two young men
d an elderly couple

Reading: a newspaper article

3 Discuss possible answers to these questions. Then read the article and compare your ideas with the information in the newspaper.

a Why do shops at London's Heathrow Airport change their displays several times a day?
b Why are retailers prepared to pay high rents for shops at Heathrow?

A shopper's paradise

IT IS MID-MORNING and expensive little shoes are on display in the Bally shop to tempt passengers waiting for a plane to Tokyo. Two hours later a flight for Nigeria is on the departure board and the showcase has changed to brightly coloured sandals in large sizes. Welcome to Heathrow, where shopping, not flying, is the largest single source of income for the British Airports Authority (BAA).

Until the late 70s passengers used to buy a bottle of whisky and a carton of cigarettes from a duty-free Skyshop and then run for their plane. Then other retailers were invited to open shops. Now passengers can buy anything from complete sound systems to designer clothes.

Retailers are helped by detailed information from the BAA. The shops are told how many passengers are passing through the airport at a particular time, and where they are going; staff then know how much people are likely to spend and what they will buy. If there is a flight to the Caribbean, for example, the shops will do well.

As a result of market research, retailers also know that first class passengers are not big spenders; because they are frequent flyers, they buy toiletries and shirts rather than luxury items. Business travellers generally spend 30 to 40 minutes in the departure area where the duty-free shops are. Foreign passengers on long-distance flights, though, arrive two hours early and spend more time in the shops. When families fly on holiday, the parents will take turns to stay with the children while one of them visits the shops.

Rents are high, but income from duty-free airport shops is growing three times faster than in the high street. 'Market research has shown us that most of our passengers want shops,' says a representative of the BAA. 'That is what we have provided.'

30

Unit 4A

4 Answer these questions about expressions from the text. Use a dictionary to help you.

a What is the main *source of income* for a shoe shop?
b What do you not have to pay if you buy something in a *duty-free shop*?
c What are *designer clothes*? What kind of person buys them in your country?
d What is the general purpose of *market research*?
e Which of these do you think are *luxury items*? What other items are luxuries?

Grammar: first conditional sentences

5 Look at this sentence from the article, and a second sentence with the same meaning. Both describe the result of a possible situation.

If there is a flight to the Caribbean, the shops will do well.

The shops will do well if there is a flight to the Caribbean.

a What will happen if there is a flight from Heathrow to the Caribbean?
b Which tense follows *if*? Which verb form is in the other part of the sentence?
c Complete these sentences with correct verb forms.
 • If my flight is delayed, I ..... shopping.
 • If I ..... hungry, I ..... a sandwich.
 • We ..... the last train if we ..... late.
 • What ..... you ..... if the plane ..... full?
 • ..... you ..... me some duty-free wine if you ..... time, please?

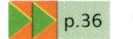 **Grammar backup 4**

Speaking: expressing possibilities and certainties

6 Look at the phrases in the *Phrasebook*.

a Which two verbs mean *will possibly*?
b Do adverbs come before or after:
 • *will*?
 • *won't*?
c Answer these questions.
 • What is your next social arrangement? What will you do if it does not happen?
 • How are you travelling home today? What will you do if that is not possible?
 • When are you going to do your English homework? What will you do if you are too busy then?

7 Work in pairs. List three groups of travellers from your country (e.g. a football team, a group of young teenagers, a professional orchestra). Then imagine that you run a large airport shop. Discuss what each group will buy. What will you display in the window?

Phrasebook

Possibilities and certainties

If all the passengers are going on holiday,
• I **definitely won't sell** many luxury items.
• we**'ll probably sell** some alcohol.
• they **might buy** swimming costumes.
• they **will certainly want** dark glasses.
• some of them **may need** shorts and T-shirts.

Retail

Action B **Around the airport**

- Listen to conversations and announcements
- Take part in service transactions
- Make requests
- Ask for a description

Listening: conversations and announcements

1 Look at the pictures A–J.
  a What do these airport staff do?
  b In which parts of the airport are they?
  c What do you think they are saying?
  d Which passengers have just arrived, do you think? Which ones are leaving?

32

Unit 4B

Speaking: service transactions

4 Work in pairs. Choose three pictures (not B or E) and act out the conversations. Use phrases from Exercise 3b and the *Phrasebook* to help you.

Speaking: asking for a description

5 Look at the picture.

2 🔊 Listen and match each extract with a picture.

3 🔊 Look at the pictures again.
a What can you remember?
   A Which bag does the customs officer want to see?
   B Where is flight IB 487 leaving from?
   C What is the airport official going to write on the form?
   D Who packed this passenger's cases?
   E Where are the passengers going now?
   F What does the security guard want?
   G What does the customer want to do?
   H What does the customer want to buy?
   I How much is a cup of coffee in the cafe?
   J When can the passenger travel?

b Match these phrases with the pictures.

charge commission	boarding passes
a detailed description	pack your bags
please go immediately	anything else
the entrance	seats available
that green case	check for you

c Listen to the extracts again and check your answers.

Phrasebook

Making requests

I'd like to buy a ticket, please.
Would you please fill in this form?
Would you mind waiting for a moment?
Can you help me, please?
Could you leave your bags here?
Please wait in line.

a What kind of bag is it?   d What colour is it?
b How long is it?   e How heavy is it?
c How wide is it?

Which type of word follows *What* in these questions? Which type of word follows *How*?

6 Complete these questions with *What* or *How*.
a ..... expensive is the ticket?
b ..... hot was it in Italy?
c ..... presents are you buying?
d ..... hungry are you?
e ..... help is given to older people?

7 Work in pairs. Act out a conversation. Then change roles.
   A: You work at the airport. Look at the lost luggage form. Ask questions to get the information that you need from the passenger.
   B: You have lost your luggage. Explain the problem to the clerk at the airport lost luggage desk.

LOST LUGGAGE FORM

NAME:

FLIGHT NUMBER: FROM:

NUMBER OF CASES:

DESCRIPTION OF CASES:

DESCRIPTION OF CONTENTS:

CONTACT ADDRESS:

33

Retail

Action C — The personal touch

- Read a newspaper article
- Change money
- Listen to a conversation at an exchange desk
- Vocabulary: currencies and financial words

Reading: a newspaper article

1 First look at the headline of the article below. Use a dictionary to help you discuss these questions.

a What is a vending machine? What do you expect to find inside one? Where do you find these machines in your country?

b Pizza and maggots are contrasted in the article. How are they different from each other? Are they surprising products for a vending machine?

2 Now read the article.

a Which of these products do *you* buy from vending machines?

b Is there anything you would *not* like to buy from one? Why not?

FROM PIZZA TO MAGGOTS

You can buy anything from a vending machine

Once it was just drinks and snacks. Now, though, there seems no limit to what you can buy from a vending machine. Hot and cold food are common – options include pizza, burgers, lasagne and chips, cooked in the machine and served hot with a choice of salt, ketchup or mayonnaise. In some hospitals disposable flower vases are sold for £1 each; this means that the hospital does not have to provide vases, and the nurses do not have to wash them up. Some fishermen are already familiar with maggot vending machines, which preserve live worms and maggots at a carefully controlled temperature and sell them in tins. They are even used to sell art. Staffordshire University displayed one full of pieces of fake wood with poems on them, at £2 each. Glasses, sunglasses, cameras and films are commonly sold this way, and recently entirely automatic stores have appeared around Europe selling anything from cigarettes to eggs to cleaning products. ■

---

3 Complete these sentences to explain words from the article. Use a dictionary to help you.

a *Common* means *not* ..... .
b *Live* means *not* ..... .
c *Fake* means *not* ..... .
d If something is *disposable*, you use it and then ..... .
e A *snack* is a ..... meal.
f *Vases* are used to display ..... .
g *Nurses* look after ..... .
h You *wash* a plate *up* because it is ..... .
i Food is *preserved* so that it does not ..... .

Speaking: machine transactions

4 Look at the picture of another kind of machine.

a What does this machine do?
b How do you use it?
c Which of these forms of money can you use?

coins   notes   cheques   credit cards

d What are the advantages and disadvantages of using a machine for this kind of transaction?

Unit 4C

Vocabulary: currencies

5 Work in pairs. Which countries use these currencies? What other currencies can you add?

pound	peso	franc
dollar	yen	mark
rouble	escudo	peseta
yuan	krona	lira

Talking point

THIS IS SILLY. IT'S TIME FOR A SINGLE WORLD CURRENCY.

What do *you* think?

Speaking and Listening: changing money

6 Work in pairs. Look at the picture sequence below.

a What do you think each person is saying? Write the conversation, and then act it out. Use these expressions to help you:

traveller's cheque exchange rate commission coin

b Listen to the conversation and compare it with your own.

c Act out a similar conversation. Change notes in your own currency into pounds.

Word file Unit 4

SHOPPING
big spender *adj + n*
market re**search** *n*
shopper *n*
showcase *n*
source of **in**come *n*
tempt *v*
vending machine *n*

PURCHASES
carton of ciga**rett**es *n*
designer **clothes** *n pl*
luxury item *n*

sound system *n*
vase *n*

FLYING
an**noun**cement *n*
boarding pass *n*
contact ad**dress** *n*
customs officer *n*
first class **pass**enger *adj + n*
frequent **fly**er *adj + n*
long-distance **flight** *adj + n*

lost luggage *n*
se**cur**ity guard *n*

MONEY
cheque *n*
coin *n*
com**miss**ion *n*
credit card *n*
ex**change** rate *n*
note *n*

FOOD
burger *n*
chips *n pl*
egg *n*
ketchup *n*

la**sa**gne *n*
mayon**naise** *n*
pizza *n*
salt *n*
snack *n*

OTHER WORDS
common *adj*
fake *adj*
live *adj*
nurse *n*
paradise *n*
pre**serve** *v*
toiletries *n pl*
wash up *v*

35

Grammar *backup 4*

First conditional sentences

Practice

1 Complete the sentences

a I'll *book* (book) the flight, if you *send* (send) the confirmation.
b Don't worry. I ..... (pay) you back when I ..... (get) my next salary cheque.
c Who ..... (get) the job if John ..... (decide) he doesn't want it?
d If my case ..... (arrive) soon, I ..... (go) to the lost luggage desk.
e Hurry up, I'm really hungry. If we ..... (go) for lunch now, we ..... (get) anything to eat.
f If you ..... (finish) the report now, your boss will be happy and he ..... (get) angry with you again.

2 Write complete sentences.

a If you / see Maria, / you / tell her about the market research meeting?
   If you see Maria, will you tell her about the market research meeting?
b I / go sailing if the weather / good at the weekend.
c What / they do if the sound system / not arrive?
d If we / phone them immediately, / lose the contract.
e If he / like the vase, he / buy it.

3 Translation

Write these sentences in your own language. Then close your Course Book. Translate the sentences back into English.

a What will you do if the weather is fine this weekend?
b I'll give him your message when I see him.
c I'll ask them about the report if I see them later today.
d If you don't book now, there won't be any seats left.

Reference

- We use the first conditional to talk about a possible situation and its result. Uses include making an offer, negotiating something and threatening someone: *If we don't leave soon, we'll miss the plane. What will you do if the plane is late? If you deliver the package by Monday, we'll sign the contract.*

- There are two parts to a conditional sentence. The *if* clause can come before or after the main clause. When the *if* clause comes second, we do not use a comma: *If we reduce our prices, we'll sell more sandals. They won't stay for a week if they don't like the hotel.*

- We can replace *will* with other modal verbs. This changes the meaning of the sentence.

	they **will** order it. (They will definitely do this.)
If the book is out of stock,	they **can** order it. (They are able to do this.)

- We can replace *if* with *when*, but the meaning of the sentence changes: *You'll understand if you see the figures.* (I don't know if you're going to see the figures. You may do.) *You'll understand when you see the figures.* (I know you're definitely going to see the figures.)

Sound check

Word stress

Same spelling, different stress

1. We can say the word *export* in two ways. Listen and read:

   EXAMPLE: ex**port** *Asian companies export a lot of electronic goods to Europe.*

   EXAMPLE: **ex**port *Japanese exports to Europe are very high.*

   What part of speech is *export* in each of the sentences?

2. There are a number of other words that follow the same stress rule.

   a Check the meanings of these words in a dictionary.

   import   increase   decrease   transport
   contract   produce   extract   insult
   progress   contrast   transfer   record

   b Practise saying the words as nouns, then as verbs. Then listen and check.

3. Choose three words from Exercise 2 and write sentences using them as nouns or verbs. Give your sentences to a partner to read aloud.

No stress

In order to stress certain parts of words, it is obvious that other parts of words are not stressed. In English, unstressed syllables often include the /ə/ sound.

1. Listen to the /ə/ sounds that are underlined in these words.

   man<u>e</u>r   work<u>er</u>   shopp<u>er</u>   wholesal<u>er</u>
   cart<u>on</u>   syst<u>em</u>

2. Practise saying the words in Exercise 1.

3. Practise saying these words. Underline the /ə/ sounds. Use a dictionary to help you.

   attend   assistant   confirm   recommend
   accurate   seasonal

4. Listen and check.

Prefixes and suffixes

1. Listen to these words. Prefixes and suffixes are <u>underlined</u>.

   <u>im</u>pat<u>ient</u>   <u>in</u>flex<u>ible</u>   <u>un</u>econom<u>ic</u>   <u>dis</u>taste<u>ful</u>
   <u>im</u>poss<u>ible</u>

   a Mark the position of the main stress for each word.

   b Do we usually stress prefixes and suffixes?

2. Practise saying these words. Then listen and check.

   untidily   improbable   uncommonly
   unsympathetic   disagreeable   disappearance

Manufacturing
On show

5

- Talk about exhibitions
- Listen to an interview
- Write a follow-up letter
- Vocabulary: exhibitions
- Grammar: revision of tenses

Action A   An international exhibition

Speaking: exhibitions

1 Look at the photographs and text below
  a When and where was this event held?
  b What happened there?
  c Have you ever been to an event like this? If so, why did you go? What did you do there?

2 Explain the meaning of these expressions connected with exhibitions. Use a dictionary to help you.

  a Who pays for:
     • a stand?   • a sample?
  b What do you do if you attend:
     • a demonstration?   • a tasting?
  c Why are these good for a buyer?
     • a discount   • a promotion
  d What is the purpose of:
     • negotiating with a seller?
     • sponsoring an event?

IFE 97

The 10th International
Food & Drink Exhibition
9–13 February 1997
London Earls Court

38

Unit 5A

Listening and Reading: an interview

3 🎧 Discuss possible answers to these questions about the exhibition in the pictures. Then listen to and read an interview with one of the exhibition organisers. Check your answers.

a Who visits this exhibition?
b Who do they meet?
c How do companies attract attention to their products?
d Why are exhibitions like this important for them?

> "There are over a thousand exhibitors here from all parts of the world. Most of the big international food and drink companies have taken a stand, and a lot of small ones too. This is a trade exhibition – it's not for members of the public. Manufacturers come here to meet buyers from other companies. It gives buyers and sellers a chance to get to know each other. Exhibitors have brought their new products here, and most of them are doing special promotions to encourage people to buy them.
>
> A lot of business is done because everybody knows you can negotiate good discounts. There are lots of events too. Earlier today there was a dragon dance sponsored by a Chinese company, and at midday a West Indian band is playing at the Caribbean food stand. And at a show like this, you don't pay for lunch! Lots of companies are doing cooking demonstrations and tastings, so there are plenty of free samples. It's an important event for anyone in the food industry. Last year's exhibition was very successful, and this year is even better."

Vocabulary: exhibitions

4 Complete the chart with nouns from the interview. Which nouns refer to people?

VERB	NOUN	VERB	NOUN
exhibit	.....	demonstrate	.....
sample	.....	taste	.....
promote	.....	sell	.....
buy	.....	manufacture	.....

Grammar: revision of tenses

5 Look at these sentences from the interview.

*Most ... companies **have taken** a stand.* (took)
*Manufacturers **come** here to meet buyers.* (are coming)
*A West Indian band **was playing** ... at eleven o'clock.* (played)

a Name the tense of each verb in bold. Why is this tense used?
b Name the tense of each verb in brackets. How does the meaning change if the verb in brackets replaces the verb in bold?
c Which tenses are used to talk about:
  • present activities? • past activities?
  • future activities?
d Make the six sentences above negative. Which tenses use the auxiliaries *do* or *did*?

▶ p.44 **Grammar backup 5**

Reading and Writing: a follow-up letter

6 Read the letter below. An exhibitor is responding to an enquiry card that was completed at the exhibition. Write a similar letter, from the same company, to the person who completed the card.

Caribbean INTERNATIONAL LTD
GEORGE AVENUE, NORWICH NR5 4ST

Mr Sharif
Unit 4, Station Estate
Worcester
May 15th

Dear Mr Sharif

Thank you for your enquiry about Caribbean International products.

I enclose information on our full range of soft drinks. If you would like to discuss any aspect of our products and pricing, please contact me at the above address and I can arrange to call on you at your convenience.

I look forward to hearing from you.

Yours sincerely

Jennifer Briton

Jennifer Briton
Sales Manager

ENQUIRY CARD — Caribbean INTERNATIONAL LTD
Name: Tony Beckett
Company: JB Supermarkets   Position: Buyer
Address: JB House, Crown Square, Cambridge CB3 8KM
Tel: 01223 566682   Fax: 01223 566683
I am interested in receiving information about the following products:
Fresh fruit juices, Fruit snack bars

Manufacturing

Action B

- Read about a company
- Listen to a conversation
- Describe personal responses
- Vocabulary:
  business activities
  emphasising adverbs
  responses to food

Good taste

Reading: introducing a company

1 Look at the texts below. Find:

a a business card.
- What is the name of the company?
- In which country is the company's head office?
- What is Karine van Geel's position there?

b an entry in an exhibition catalogue.
- What does the company produce?
- How many company representatives are at the exhibition?
- Why are they attending it?

c an introduction to the company.
- How old is the company?
- What is special about its products?

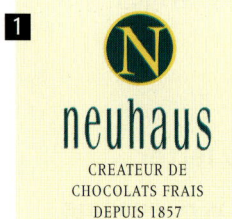

1

neuhaus
CREATEUR DE CHOCOLATS FRAIS DEPUIS 1857

Karine VAN GEEL
MARKETING MANAGER

POSTWEG 2/B • 1602 VLEZENBEEK (BELGIUM)
TEL. 32 2/568.22.11 • FAX. 32 2/568.22.07-08

2

neuhaus

Neuhaus: quality, innovation, and fine taste

When it comes to the delicious world of fine chocolate, one master chocolatier stands out, Neuhaus. Chocolate makers since 1857 and creators of Praline, Neuhaus is the oldest chocolate house in Belgium and still one of the most innovative.

3

BDBH / OBCE

3341/14

Neuhaus
Postweg 2
B - 1602 VLEZENBEEK

Delegates: Mr. R. VAN COPPENOLLE
            Mrs K. VAN GEEL
            Mr. B. MOORE

Phone: +322 568.22.11
Fax: +322 568.22.07

– Belgian chocolates, pralines, chocolate bars, tablets, or any chocolate related product

At IFE'98 we will be looking for contacts with:
– distributors
– retailers
– buyers from department stores and supermarkets
– catering contractors.

Vocabulary: business activities

2 Match these definitions to words in the texts.

a people who manage shops
b people who buy products for a chain of shops
c companies that supply shops with goods
d companies that provide food and drink for events or for other businesses

Unit 5B

Listening to a conversation

3 🔊 Look at the photograph.

a Describe what is happening.
b Listen to the conversation. What does the man like about the chocolate?

4 🔊 Listen again.

a What is a Caprice chocolate made from?
b Complete the man's responses to the chocolate.
   It looks ..... . It's ...., absolutely ...., and it tastes so ..... .
c What words can replace *absolutely* in the sentence above?
d Imagine that the man did not like the chocolate. Change his comments.

Vocabulary: responses to food

5 Look at this chart. Which adjectives express negative responses to food? Use a dictionary to help you. Can you add other words?

General	Look	Taste / Smell	Taste
beautiful	unattractive	disgusting	fresh
wonderful	pretty	delicious	stale
terrible		foul	milky
fantastic			bitter
awful			sweet
incredible			nutty
lovely			spicy
unpleasant			creamy
nice			

Vocabulary: emphasising adverbs

6 Some adverbs like *absolutely*, are used with strong adjectives like *delicious*. Others emphasise less strong adjectives. Ask and answer questions about a – d. Use words from the chart.

EXAMPLE: **A:** *Did you enjoy your last holiday?*
B: *No, it was extremely boring.*

absolutely simply really	delicious awful terrible amazing incredible fantastic

really very extremely	boring pretty nice exciting difficult enjoyable unpleasant

a a holiday   c a social event
b a film   d a work or school activity

7 Compare the forms of these responses. What part of speech follows *like*?

- It tastes awful.
- It tastes like cardboard.

Speaking: personal responses

8 Look at the pictures and work in pairs. Discuss your responses to these situations. Use expressions from the *Phrasebook*.

Phrasebook

Describing responses

It looks beautiful.
It's wonderful.
It tastes bitter.
It smells good.
It looks like a painting.
It tastes like sand.
It smells like old socks.
It was wonderful, **absolutely** fantastic.

Manufacturing

Action C

- Talk about specifications
- Read promotional signs
- Listen to a conversation
- Make a sale
- Grammar: comparisons and degrees of difference

Best buys

Speaking: specifications

1 Work in pairs. Imagine you are looking for a new portable computer at a computer exhibition. Which of these qualities do you think are most important? Are there other features that you should look for?

It should be ...	light inexpensive fast modern reliable powerful
It should have ...	a big memory a long guarantee a large screen a full-size keyboard

Reading promotional signs

2 Look at these signs from exhibition stands, and answer the questions.

> There's never been a portable as fast as ours.

a Are there faster portables?
b Which expression means 'equally fast'?

> **THE LIGHTEST PORTABLE IN THE WORLD!**
> Considerably lighter than our competitors' machines.

c Which expression means 'much lighter'?

> If you can find a less expensive portable PC than this one, we will refund DOUBLE the difference!

d Does the company believe that cheaper portables exist?
e Which expression means 'cheaper'?

3 Look at the chart in Exercise 5. Are these statements true or false? Correct the false ones.

a The DOT 200 is *the most expensive* machine.
b The GATE 166 is *a lot heavier than* the PIXEL 166.
c The PIXEL 166 is *not as fast as* the PACEMAKER 200.
d The battery life of the PACEMAKER 200 is *the shortest*.
e The PIXEL 166 *has a bigger hard disk than* the GATE 166.

42

Unit **5C**

Grammar: comparisons

4 Look back at the comparisons in Exercises 2 and 3.

a Complete this table with appropriate forms of the adjectives.

Adjective	Comparative	Superlative
light	.....	.....
expensive	.....	.....
cheap	.....	the cheapest
powerful	.....	.....
heavy	.....	the heaviest
short	shorter	the shortest
big	.....	the biggest

b Complete the following with appropriate forms of the adjective *cheap*.
  • 'This machine is considerably ..... than that one, but it's not as ..... as the one we saw in the magazine. That was ..... of all.'

c Now complete the same text with forms of the adjective *powerful*.

5 Work in pairs. Write five more comparisons between the portables in the chart below. Use expressions from the *Phrasebook*.

	GATE 166	PIXEL 166	DOT 200	PACEMAKER 200
Price	£1800	£1750	£2250	£2299
Hard disk	850Mb	1Gb	1.6Gb	2Gb
Memory	16Mb	16Mb	32Mb	32Mb
Speed	166Mhz	166Mhz	200Mhz	200Mhz
Weight	3Kg	3.5Kg	2.2Kg	3Kg
Battery life	6 hours	6 hours	5 hours	3 hours
Notes	10% discount at exhibition. 1 year's free maintenance	2 years' free maintenance at exhibition	Free fax modem at exhibition. 1 year's free maintenance	Free leather carrying case. 1 year's free maintenance

Phrasebook

Degrees of difference

Ours is **a little** smaller.
It's **considerably** lighter.
It's got a **much** bigger memory.
The screen is **far** larger.
It's **a lot** easier to use.

Listening and Speaking: making a sale

6 Listen to a conversation between a salesperson at an exhibition and a customer. Answer the questions.

a Which of the computers in the chart in Exercise 5 are they talking about?
b Who is in control of the conversation?
c How much will the customer pay if she buys the machine?

7 Work in pairs.
  A: You are the salesperson on the PACEMAKER stand. Try to persuade your customer to buy the PACEMAKER 200 portable.
  B: You are a customer. You have looked at the DOT 200 and you are unsure whether to buy that machine or a PACEMAKER. Ask questions and then make a decision.

Word file Unit 5

EXHIBITIONS
buyer *n*
catalogue entry *n*
catering
    contractor *n*
demonstrate *v*
demon**stra**tion *n*
dis**trib**utor *n*
ex**hib**it *n*
ex**hib**itor *n*
pro**mote** *v*
pro**mo**tion *n*
range *n*
re**tail**er *n*
sample *n*
sponsor *n*
tasting *n*

FEATURES
inex**pen**sive *adj*
innovation *n*
innovative *adj*
powerful *adj*

quality *n*
re**li**able *adj*
specifi**ca**tion *n*
speed *n*
weight *n*

RESPONSES
de**li**cious *adj*
dis**gust**ing *adj*
fan**tas**tic *adj*
foul *adj*
in**cred**ible *adj*
pretty *adj*
terrible *adj*

QUALITIES
bitter *adj*
creamy *adj*
fresh *adj*
milky *adj*
nutty *adj*
smell *v*
spicy *adj*

stale *adj*
sweet *adj*
taste *v*

COMPUTERS
discount *n*
guar**an**tee *n*
hard disk *n*
keyboard *n*
maintenance *n*
memory *n*
modem *n*
portable *n/adj*
screen *n*

ADVERBS OF DEGREE
absolutely *adv*
con**sid**erably *adv*
ex**treme**ly *adv*
really *adv*
simply *adv*
unbe**liev**ably *adv*

▶ p.45 Grammar backup 5

Grammar backup 5

Revision of tenses

Practice

1 Choose the correct form.

a I am *visiting* / *visit* him this evening.
b Francis writes / is writing a report at the moment.
c I meet / am meeting her for lunch tomorrow at one o'clock.
d They haven't arrived / don't arrive yet.
e Has she visited / Did she visit the office last week?
f We meet / have met before but I can't remember when.
g She lives / has lived in London all her life.

2 Complete the sentences with the correct form of the verb in brackets.

a He never *arrives* (arrive) at work before ten o'clock.
b They ..... (have) this house since 1978.
c I can't find the report. ..... (you / see) it?
d She ..... (send) a fax when the fax machine stopped working.
e I ..... (buy) her a present. Would you like to see it?
f We ..... (attend) the conference several times in the last five years.
g They ..... (live) in a flat in Oxford until next year.

3 Translation
Write these sentences in your own language. Then close your Course Book. Translate the sentences back into English.

a I'm working hard at the moment.
b They were having a meeting when I arrived.
c He's worked for the bank for ten years.
d She's just left the office.
e You've travelled to a lot of countries, haven't you?

Reference

- The present simple is used for permanent situations, routine actions and habits: *I **live** in Madrid. He **doesn't travel** to work by bus. **Does** she **visit** her mother every Sunday?*

- The present continuous is used for future arrangements with a specific time, actions which are happening at the moment of speaking, and present temporary situations: *I**'m seeing** them this evening. They **aren't working** now. **Is** she **living** in Madrid at the moment?*

- The past simple is used to talk about activities, situations and events which were completed in the past at a specific time: ***Did** they **go** on holiday yesterday? He **talked** to the manager last week.*

- The past continuous is used for activities happening in the past which were temporary, simultaneous or interrupted: *A band **was playing** earlier. I **was writing** a letter while they **were finishing** the report. They **were talking** to Franco when the phone rang.*

- The present perfect simple links the past and present. It is used to talk about past events which have no specific past time marker, have a present result, continue to the present or have not happened yet: *They**'ve met** several times. **Have** you **finished** the report? Yes, here it is. She**'s been** in the meeting for three hours. He **hasn't phoned** yet.*

Comparative and superlative adjectives, *as* + adj + *as*

Practice

1 Write the comparative and superlative forms.

a intelligent — *more intelligent* — *most intelligent*
b wet — ..... — .....
c spicy — ..... — .....
d incredible — ..... — .....
e safe — ..... — .....
f sweet — ..... — .....
g bad — ..... — .....

2 Look at the notes comparing two offices. Complete the report.

<u>Park Lane</u>
– 4 rooms
– rent / £2000 pm
– light
– attractive / newly decorated

<u>Fleet Street</u>
– 3 rooms
– rent / £1000 pm
– convenient / close to underground
– good facilities

I've seen both offices now. The one in Park Lane is (a) *larger / bigger* with four rooms but the rent is (b) ..... at £2000 per month. However, with so many windows, it is (c) ....., and it is (d) ..... because it is newly decorated. The office in Fleet Street is not as (e) ..... the first one because it only has three rooms but it is (f) ..... at £1000 per month. It is also (g) ..... because it is (h) ..... to the underground station. In fact, it has (i) ..... facilities ...... the one in Park Lane. So I think we should rent the one in Fleet Street for six months.

3 Translation

Write these sentences in your own language. Then close your Course Book. Translate the sentences back into English.

a My country has the best weather.
b E-mails are far more convenient than faxes.
c Planes are as comfortable as trains.

Reference

- To compare the qualities of two things, we can use comparative adjectives. To compare the qualities of three or more things in a group, we can use superlative adjectives.

	Adjective	Comparative	Superlative
One syllable	fast	fast**er** (than)	(the) fast**est**
One syllable, ending in vowel + consonant	big	big**ger** (than)	(the) big**gest**
Two or more syllables	expensive	**more** expensive (than)	the **most** expensive
Two syllables ending in *y*	heavy	heav**ier** (than)	(the) heav**iest**

- Irregular adjectives include: *good, better, best; bad, worse, worst; far, further, furthest*.

- We never use *very* with a comparative adjective. We use words like *much, far, a lot, considerably* and *a little* to describe the amount of difference: *French trains are* **much** *faster than English ones; Maria is* **far** *more efficient than Monica*.

- We use *as* + adj + *as* to talk about things which are the same / equal in some way. We add *not* if the relationship is unequal: *Faxes are* **as** *quick* **as** *e-mails.* (They take the same time to arrive.) *Letters are* **not as** *quick* **as** *e-mails.* (They take more time to arrive.)

Manufacturing
On the market

6

Action A — Neuhaus Mondose

- Read an introduction to a company
- Vocabulary: compound words
- Grammar: defining relative clauses

Reading an introduction to a company

1 Discuss these questions.

a What are your favourite chocolates?
b Where do they come from?
c Which company makes them?
d What other chocolate manufacturers can you name?

2 Read an introduction to Neuhaus Mondose.

a When and where was the first shop opened?
b What three things did Neuhaus invent?
c Where are Neuhaus Mondose's main markets?
d What do the photographs show?

Neuhaus Mondose makes high quality luxury Belgian chocolates that are known by chocolate lovers all over the world. The first shop was opened, in the centre of Brussels, by Jean Neuhaus in 1857. The company is now the oldest confectioner in the world that still produces hand-made chocolates. When people think of Belgian chocolates they think of the chocolate *praline*, a mixture of chocolate, sugar and almonds. The Neuhaus family created the first praline; they were also the first to make chocolates which had rich fillings covered by a chocolate shell.

Neuhaus also invented the *ballotin*. In the early 1900s chocolates were sold in small bags and the ones at the bottom of the bag were often damaged. The ballotin protects the chocolates, and it has become the traditional packaging for loose Belgian chocolates.

Neuhaus Mondose is no longer a family business, but it is still Belgian-owned. The company has a turnover of over 1.6 billion Belgian francs (about $60 million) each year, and exports its products worldwide. Europe, the United States and Japan are the markets where Neuhaus Mondose products sell best. The chocolates are sold in special Neuhaus shops, in well-known department stores (like Harrods, El Corte Ingles and Sachs Fifth Avenue) and in duty-free shops at airports. People who buy them know they are buying some of the world's finest chocolates.

46

Unit 6A

3 Match the halves of sentences to explain the word in *italics*.

a A *confectioner* ... ... is the place where it sells most.
b A *damaged* item ... ... protects a product.
c *Packaging* ... ... sells a wide variety of goods.
d A *loose* chocolate ... ... can move freely in its container.
e A company's *turnover* ... ... makes or sells sweets.
f A company's main *market* ... ... is broken or of poor quality.
g A *department store* ... ... is the amount of business that it does.

Vocabulary: compound words

4 Look at these words from the text:

hand-made – made by hand
duty-free – without tax
worldwide – all over the world

Make words that mean:

a made in a factory
b without sugar
c all over the nation
d all over Europe
e without paying rent
f made by machine

Grammar: defining relative clauses

5 Look at these sentences from the text.

*The company is now the oldest confectioner in the world **that still produces hand-made chocolates**.*

a Is there an older company producing hand-made chocolates?
b Is the company the oldest confectioner in the world?
c What does *that* refer to?

*Europe, the United States and Japan are the markets **where Neuhaus products sell best**.*

d Are Neuhaus products only sold in these places?
e What does *where* refer to?

6 Look for other relative clauses in the text beginning with *that, where, which* and *who*. Which relative pronouns refer to:

a people?
b places?
c things?

7 Complete these sentences with a relative pronoun.

a These are the chocolates ..... sell best in Britain.
b She's the woman ..... manages the company in France.
c Neuhaus uses nuts ..... are imported from the United States.
d The factory ..... the chocolates are made is just outside Brussels.
e The box ..... Neuhaus invented is used by many Belgian chocolate companies.

▶▶ p.52 Grammar backup 6

8 In an ideal world, what kind of company would you like to work for? Complete these sentences for yourself, then discuss them with the group. Be ready to give reasons.

EXAMPLE: *I'd like to work for a company that ...*
I'd like to work for a boss who ...
I'd like to work in a place where ...

Talking point

IT DOESN'T MATTER TO ME WHAT THE COMPANY MAKES. IT'S JUST A JOB.

What do *you* think?

Manufacturing

Action B **Products**

- Listen to a description of a product range
- Describe objects and products
- Listen to an interview
- Vocabulary:
  containers
  shapes

Vocabulary: containers

1 Answer questions about these words for containers. Use a dictionary to help you.

| bag | barrel | box | carton | jar | packet | sack | tin | tube |

a   What is each type of container made of?
b   What kind of food or drink is sold in these containers?
c   Which containers are used as packaging in the photographs above?

Listening to a description of a product range

2 🔊 Listen to an extract from an interview with Karine Van Geel, Marketing Manager of Neuhaus Mondose. In which order does she refer to the products in the pictures above?

3 🔊 Listen again.
a   How are ballotins priced?
b   Which picture shows the 'napolitain'?
c   Which product is often sold to hotels and airlines?

48

Unit **6B**

6 Identify these objects.

a It's long and rectangular. It's usually made of plastic. It's marked in centimetres.
b They're made of leather, wool, cotton or rubber. They're made in the shape of your hand.

Speaking: describing objects

7 Think of an object and describe it to the class. Stop after each sentence to let the others guess what the object is.

Listening to an interview

8 Discuss these questions.

a What kind of people do you think buy Neuhaus chocolates?
b Do you think there are national preferences for different kinds of chocolates, or do we all like the same ones?

9 Listen to the first part of another interview with Karine.

a Are these statements true or false? Correct the false ones.
 • The main buyers of Neuhaus chocolates in duty-free shops are women.
 • The average Neuhaus customer is quite old.
 • Neuhaus chocolates are expensive.
 • The company wants to sell more to children.
b Describe a typical Neuhaus customer.

10 Listen to the second part. Match the people with their preferences for types of chocolate.

PEOPLE	CHOCOLATES
Europeans	big
Germans	white
Americans	in boxes
Japanese	individual
Arabs	wrapped
Britons	unwrapped
French	dark and bitter
	sweet and milky

Vocabulary: shapes

4 Look at the shapes.

1. circle 2. square 3. oval
4. triangle 5. heart 6. rectangle

a Match these words to the shapes. Use a dictionary to help you.

> oval   round   rectangular   square
> heart-shaped   triangular

b Find chocolates in the pictures above and opposite with these shapes.

5 Draw the objects described below to show your understanding of the phrases. Then compare your drawings with a partner's.

a an L-shaped room
b a star-shaped mirror
c a mushroom-shaped table
d a six-sided / hexagonal coin
e a chocolate in the shape of a dollar sign
f a greetings card shaped like a flower

Speaking and Writing: describing a product

11 Work in pairs. Choose a food or drink product that you both know well.

a Discuss the shape, size, packaging, country of origin, taste, ingredients, and type of purchaser. Make notes.
b Write a paragraph about the product based on your notes.

Manufacturing

Action C

- Talk about market research
- Interpret data
- Explain changes
- Vocabulary:
  fast food outlets
  verbs used to describe changes

Market research

Speaking: market research

1 Work in pairs. Discuss these questions.

a What is market research? How does it help a business?
b Imagine you are starting a company to produce one of these:
   - a new magazine
   - sports shoes
   - portable televisions

   What market information do you need?

Reading and Speaking: interpreting data

2 Study the table below.

a What is fast food?
b Which fast food outlets sell the food in the pictures on these pages?
c Did fast food sales grow in Britain between 1991 and 1995?
d Fish and chips are traditional British fast food. Were they the most popular fast food in 1995?

Phrasebook

Interpreting data

Sales **increased / rose slightly** in 1994.
Sales **remained at the same level**.
Sales **fell / decreased sharply** between 1991 and 1995.
The market **grew / expanded dramatically**.
The market **shrank / got smaller** in 1992.

Market size for fast food 1991–95 (£m) in Britain

FAST FOOD OUTLETS	1991	1992	1993	1994	1995
Hamburger bars	920	950	1020	1100	1190
Fried chicken restaurants	280	285	290	310	325
Pizzerias	610	640	680	710	745
Fish & chip shops	680	670	670	680	690
Sandwich bars, bakeries and cafes	1500	1550	1620	1740	1830
Chinese take-aways	340	350	350	350	355
Indian take-aways	235	250	265	275	285
Other	105	100	105	110	120
TOTAL	4670	4795	5000	5275	5540

Unit **6C**

3 Look at these statements based on information from the table.
- Chinese take-away food sales increased very little between 1991 and 1995.
- The market for pizzas grew by £35 million in 1995.
- Fish and chip sales fell from £680 million to £670 million in 1992.

a Make statements about these foods. Use the *Phrasebook* on page 50 to help you.
- Indian take-away food, 1995
- Fish and chips, 1993
- Pizzas, 1991–1995
- Hamburgers, 1995
- Total fast food sales, 1991–1995

b Do you think the data for your country is similar? Why (not)?

4 Work in pairs. Imagine you want to open a fast food restaurant or take-away in Britain. Using information from the table, decide which type of food to sell. Explain your choice.

Speaking and Listening: explaining changes

5 Look at some reasons people give for the rising popularity of fast food. Can you explain how each one might affect fast food sales?

a The changing roles of women.
b The trend away from full family meals.
c The length of the working day, including long travelling times.
d The rising number of single-person households.
e Children's expectations about food.

6 Listen to five people explaining why they eat a lot of fast food. Match their reasons with the explanations in Exercise 5.

Speaking and Writing: interpreting data

7 Look at the table below.

a Summarise the most important changes in the sales of these drinks.
b Write sentences suggesting reasons for the trends.

Drinks in British homes 1984–94
(% of population)

	Tea	Coffee	Soft drinks
1984	84.1	60.4	43.9
1986	82.0	60.1	46.6
1988	81.4	58.3	49.0
1990	80.1	57.6	51.8
1992	78.7	56.9	53.7
1994	77.1	55.9	55.7

Word file Unit 6

FOOD PRODUCTS
almond *n*
bar *n*
con**fec**tioner *n*
filling *n*
hand-made *adj*
indi**vid**ual *adj*
loose *adj*
packaging *n*
wrap *v*
(**un**)**wrapped** *adj*

CONTAINERS
barrel *n*
carton *n*
jar *n*
sack *n*
tin *n*
tube *n*

SHAPES
heart-shaped *adj*
hex**ag**onal *adj*
oval *adj*
rec**tang**ular *adj*
round *adj*
square *adj*
tri**ang**ular *adj*

FAST FOOD
fish and **chips** *n*
fried chicken
    adj + n
hamburger *n*
outlet *n*
sandwich *n*
take-away *n*

OTHER WORDS
damaged *adj*
de**part**ment
    store *n*
market *n*
trend *n*
turnover *n*
world**wide** *adv*

Grammar backup 6

Defining relative clauses

Practice

1 Write sentences a – e as single sentences. Use a relative clause to include information from the second sentence.

a I want to see the report. They sent the report this morning.
I want to see the report that they sent this morning.
b That is the man. I met him at the conference last week.
c This is the office. I moved into it last month.
d I'm sure this is the street. I parked my car in this street this morning.
e I have a friend. Her boss speaks ten languages!

2 Correct the mistake in each sentence. Do not change the meaning of the sentence.

a I enjoy working with people ~~whose~~ *who* are flexible.
b Let's go to that Spanish restaurant who the staff are so helpful.
c I always listen to people who ideas are good.
d I remember the time which the company made a loss.
e I like people which are sympathetic.
f This is the awful tablecloth when I bought on holiday.
g I like people who they are friendly.

3 Which sentences can omit the relative pronoun?

a That's the manager (who) I've met before.
b The staff who work in central London often have long journeys to work.
c The faxes which arrived yesterday contain very important information.
d The holiday that they've just booked is very expensive.
e The meal that we had last night was delicious.
f This is the tourist agency where I booked my ticket.

4 Translation

Write these sentences in your own language. Then close your Course Book. Translate the sentences back into English.

a This is the house where I lived as a child.
b I have a friend whose son works in my department.
c I've lost the report you sent me yesterday.
d The watch which I bought yesterday doesn't work.

Reference

- Relative clauses give more information about a person or thing.
- Defining relative clauses identify which person or thing we mean. Without the clause, the sentence loses essential information and sometimes does not make sense: *People **who work hard** earn more money.*
- Non-defining relative clauses give extra information about people or things. They have two commas which separate the clause from the rest of the sentence: *The company**, which has its head office in Geneva,** employs 600 people.*
- Defining relative clauses usually start with a relative pronoun:

who / whom	people	They're the people **who** I met last week.
which	things	The chocolates **which** they sell are hand-made.
that	people or things (less formal than 'who' or 'which')	The chocolates **that** they sell are hand-made. They're the people **that** I met last week.
whose	people or things 'possessive'	She's the person **whose** job I want.
where	place	The hotel **where** I stayed is very expensive.

- *Who*, *which* and *that* can be used as the subject or object of a relative clause:
Subject: *The machine **which** arrived yesterday is very modern.*
Object: *The machine **which** we've ordered is very modern.*
- We can leave out *that*, *who*, or *which* when they are the object in the relative clause: *The people **(who)** I saw gave me some good advice.*
- We can use *whom* instead of *who* as the object of the relative clause, although it is no longer common in spoken English. *The man **whom** I met was French.*

Sound check

Sounds and spelling

Silent letters

A number of common words in English contain 'silent letters'. It is hard to give any general rules; it is better simply to learn the pronunciation of particular words. Here are some of the most common.

1. Listen and repeat the words below. Which letters are not pronounced?

know	knife	knee	knock		
write	wrong	wrap	typewriter		
campaign	foreign	sign	champagne		
would	could	should	calm	talk	walk
comb	lamb	bomb	limb		
light	weigh	straight	through		

2. Now practise saying the words.

Words with *ough*

The letters *ough* are pronounced in a number of different ways.

1. How many of these words can you pronounce? Practise saying them. Then listen and repeat.

A	B	C	D	E
through	although	cough	bought	rough
	though		thought	tough
			fought	enough
			nought	

2. Match the vowel sounds in each of the words below with the sounds in the columns above.

a o<u>ff</u>   b sh<u>or</u>t   c wh<u>o</u>   d s<u>o</u>   e st<u>u</u>ff

'Missing' syllables

A lot of English three and four-syllable words are shortened when we speak; syllables that seem to be there in the spelling often 'disappear' completely.

1. Listen to these words and underline the letters that seem to disappear.

business   interesting   different   chocolate   temperature   frightening

2. Mark the main stress above each word.

3. Practise saying the words. Then listen again and check.

Manufacturing
In production

7

Action A

- Read about production processes
- Listen to a description of a production process
- Describe a production process
- Grammar: present perfect passive

Processes

Reading and Speaking: production processes

1 How do you think individual chocolates are made? Discuss possible methods.

2 Read an extract from a factory tour. What is the main characteristic of the 'enrobing' process?

> 'We're particularly famous for our hand-made chocolates. For many of these we use a process called *enrobing*. That means that we make the centre first, by hand. Then we pour liquid chocolate over it. The Caprice is a good example of an enrobed hand-made chocolate. The chocolate in the outer covering is made to a secret recipe. It arrives here as a liquid and remains like that until we use it in the manufacturing process.'

3 Read the text opposite, 'Producing the Caprice', and look at the photographs of the production process below.

a Put the pictures in the order that they are described in the text.
b How are the verb forms in the text different from those in the text in Exercise 2? Explain the reasons for the difference.

54

Unit **7A**

Grammar: present perfect passive

4 Find three examples of the present perfect passive in the text below.

a Explain how the present perfect passive is formed.
b When can we use the present perfect passive in process descriptions?

5 These words were spoken on a factory tour. Rewrite them using passive verb forms.

a We bring liquid chocolate to the factory in lorries.
b After he has made the filling, we take it to the cool room.
c We import the nuts from the US.
d He's decorated these, and now we send them through the cooling tunnel.
e We keep the factory kitchen clean.

▶▶ p.60 **Grammar backup 7**

Speaking and Listening: describing a production process

6 Neuhaus also use a process called 'moulding', for chocolates with soft centres.

a What do you think the process involves? Use these words to help you:

| shell | filling | liquid chocolate | mould |

b Listen and make notes about the process.
c Explain the main difference between *moulding* and *enrobing*.
d Describe the stages in the moulding process. Use some of the sequence words below and the present perfect passive if it is appropriate.

| First (of all) | then | after | when | finally |

7 Describe a production process that you have seen or heard about.

Producing the Caprice

First of all, the mixture for the centre is prepared in the factory kitchen and poured on to a conveyor belt. The soft mixture is cut into squares and then sent through a cooling tunnel. After the squares have been cooled, they are taken off the conveyor and put in trays. Then they are placed on a heated table and each one is folded by hand. After they have been folded, they are filled with fresh cream. Then they are passed under a curtain of liquid chocolate and tiny rollers coat the bottom of each piece. When they have been passed through the cooling tunnel and the shell is hard, they are packed and weighed.

55

Manufacturing

Action B

The right approach

- Listen to and describe qualities for a job
- Vocabulary:
  factory jobs
  personal qualities and skills
- Grammar:
  adverbs

Vocabulary: factory jobs

1 Look at the photographs below.

a Where is each person working? What are they doing?
b Match these job titles with the pictures:

packer   machine operator
production manager   assembler
quality control manager

Listening: qualities for a job

2 Listen. How does the speaker finish the sentences below?

A good packer should be able to ..... .
A good packer should be ..... .
A good packer should have ..... .

Vocabulary: personal qualities and skills

3 Look at the phrases in Exercise 4 and use a dictionary. Which words or phrases are about:

a money?
b time?
c organisation?
d relationships?
e management?
f knowledge and interests?
g other areas?

56

4 Choose phrases from the table below that you think are relevant to the people in the photographs opposite. Give reasons for your choices.

EXAMPLE: *I think a quality control manager should have an interest in science because a lot of the work involves scientific tests.*

1 should have ...	2 should be ...	3 should be able to ...
a desire to do a good job	a good leader	plan carefully
planning skills	calm	solve problems calmly
financial skills	good with figures	do repetitive tasks accurately
technical understanding	strong and fit	work fast
good timekeeping	neat	concentrate easily
an interest in science	reliable	work hard
good communication skills	punctual	work independently
	patient	work well as part of a team
	clean	make decisions quickly
	a fast worker	

Grammar: adverbs

5 Look at these two phrases from the table above:

... should be a **good** leader
... should be able to plan **carefully**

a The adjective *good* describes a quality of a leader. What does the adverb *carefully* describe?
b Adjectives tell us more about nouns. What do adverbs tell us more about?
c Find all the adverbs in column 3 and complete the table below. How are regular adverbs formed?

	Regular					Irregular			
adjective	careful	calm	accurate	independent	quick	easy	good	fast	hard
adverb									

6 Complete these sentences with an adverb.
a In a difficult situation I always behave ..... .
b I can speak English ..... .
c When I have to make an important decision I make it ..... .
d I hate it when other people drive ..... .
e If you're talking to a foreigner it's best to speak ..... .

▶▶ p.61 **Grammar backup 7**

Speaking: describing qualities for a job

7 Work in pairs. Choose one of the factory jobs. Decide which of you is better for the job and why.

8 Describe the qualities that you need to do *your* job, or a job that you would like to have.

Talking point

THIS IS WHAT BEING A GOOD LEADER MEANS TO ME ... I TELL THEM WHAT TO DO AND THEY OBEY ME.

What do *you* think?

Manufacturing

Action C

- Discuss job responsibilities
- Read about a job
- Listen to a description of a product sheet
- Read and write faxes and accompanying letters
- Vocabulary: phrases of purpose, reason and result

Product specifications

Speaking: job responsibilities

1 Which of the people (a – e) below is interested in each of these specifications of a ballotin of Neuhaus chocolates?
   - the number and type of chocolates
   - the weight of the chocolates
   - the weight of the packaging
   - the type of packaging
   - the shelf-life of the chocolates
   - the number of ballotins in a carton
   - the number of cartons on a pallet
   - the alcohol content
   - the price

   a a customer in a shop
   b a customs officer
   c a storeman
   d a manager of a shop in the US
   e a marketing manager of a hotel

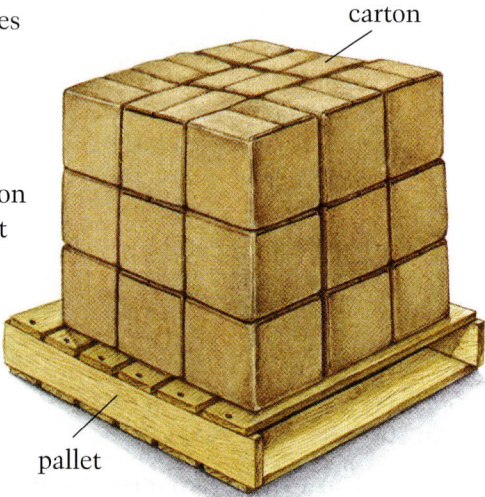

Reading about a job

2 Read about Sylvia Devogeleer's job at Neuhaus.
   a Compare your answers to Exercise 1 with what she says.
   b How can you recognise a good product sheet?

> "An important part of my job is to prepare information sheets about each of our products. The purpose of these is to give detailed information about our products to customers. People like shop managers in other countries, and hotel chains who want to give away Neuhaus chocolates, need to know what a particular ballotin or box contains. Then if we send loose chocolates and empty ballotins, they also need to know how to fill them – and about the shelf-life of the chocolates. Some people need more information about the ingredients that are in the chocolates. Customers in Kuwait, for example, want to know about the alcohol content. The reason why this is important is that alcohol can't be imported into Kuwait. Then there are details about transportation and storage, the number of mini ballotins in a carton, how big each carton is, how many cartons go on a pallet. The result is that retailers can assemble each product correctly and consistently."

Vocabulary: phrases of reason, purpose and result

3 Look at these sentences from the text.

   The purpose of these is to give detailed information about our products to customers.
   The reason why this is important is that alcohol can't be imported into Kuwait.
   The result is that retailers can assemble each product correctly and consistently.

   a Notice the structures that follow the words in bold.
   b Which part of each sentence explains the purpose, the reason or the result?

58

Unit **7C**

4 Now finish these sentences in the same way

a The reason why I live in my town ..... .
b The result of working hard ..... .
c The purpose of studying English ..... .

Listening to a description of a product sheet

5 🎧 Sylvia is describing the kind of information on a product sheet. Listen and complete the table below.

Product	Mini Ballotin	Total weight	.....
No. of chocolates	.....	Shelf-life	.....
Weight of chocolates	.....	No. of mini ballotins in a carton	.....

Reading and writing faxes and accompanying letters

6 Look at this fax that Sylvia received and the letter that she wrote in reply.

a Which country is the fax from?
b What did Sylvia include with her letter?

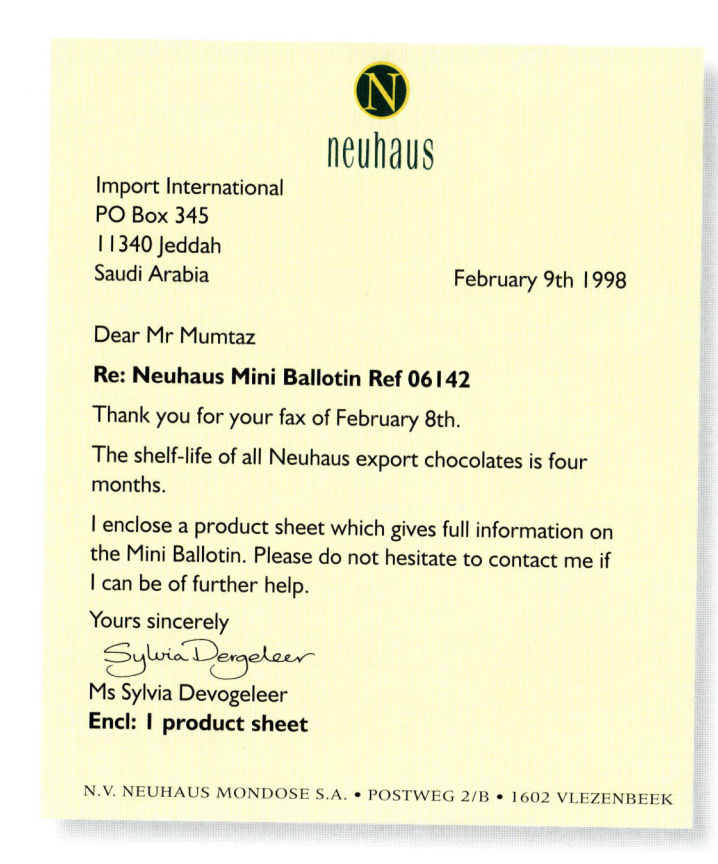

Import International   Page 1

FAX

To: Ms Sylvia Devogeleer
         Neuhaus Mondose

From: Mr A. Mumtaz
         Import International
         PO Box 345
         11340 Jeddah
         Saudi Arabia.

Date: February 8th   **Pages:** 1

Re: Neuhaus Mini Ballotin Ref 06142

Could you please send information on the above product. We particularly need to know about the shelf-life of the chocolates.

Yours sincerely

A. Mumtaz

A. Mumtaz

---

neuhaus

Import International
PO Box 345
11340 Jeddah
Saudi Arabia   February 9th 1998

Dear Mr Mumtaz

Re: Neuhaus Mini Ballotin Ref 06142

Thank you for your fax of February 8th.

The shelf-life of all Neuhaus export chocolates is four months.

I enclose a product sheet which gives full information on the Mini Ballotin. Please do not hesitate to contact me if I can be of further help.

Yours sincerely

Sylvia Devogeleer

Ms Sylvia Devogeleer

Encl: 1 product sheet

N.V. NEUHAUS MONDOSE S.A. • POSTWEG 2/B • 1602 VLEZENBEEK

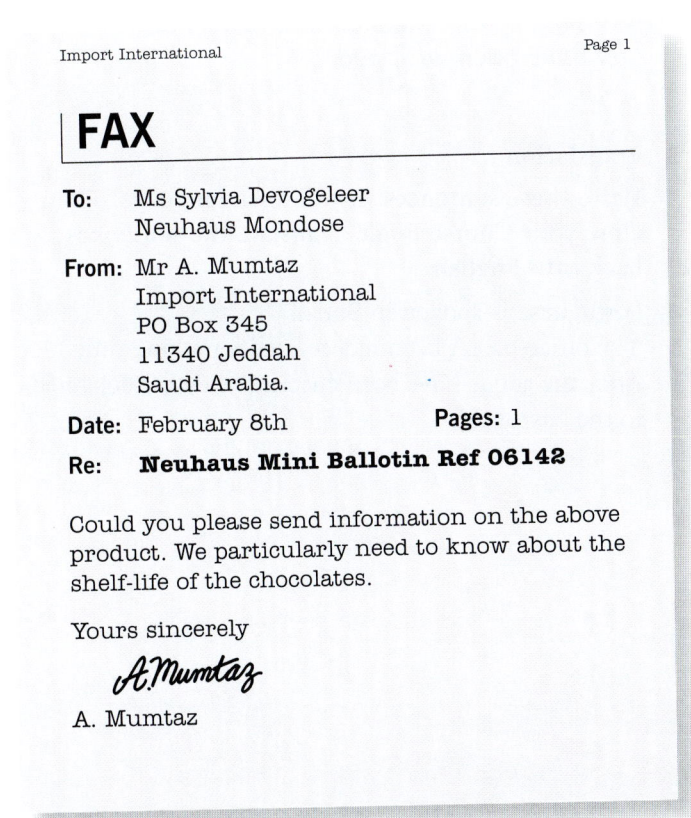

7 Write a fax to Sylvia asking for information about the Tins Collection. You are interested in the weight of the Garden tin and the number of tins in a carton. Then exchange faxes with your partner. Write a letter to reply to your partner's fax and say that you are including a product sheet.
(The Garden tin is 400 grams – 10 tins per carton.)

Word file Unit 7

FOOD PRODUCTION	FACTORIES	KNOWLEDGE, SKILLS AND QUALITIES
centre *n*	**con**veyor belt *n*	
coat *v*	**roll**er *n*	**ac**curate *adj*
covering *n*	**PRODUCT SPECIFICATION**	calm *adj*
decorate *v*		communi**ca**tion skills *n pl*
fill *v*	**al**cohol content *n*	**con**centrate *v*
fold *v*	**la**bel *n*	con**sis**tently *adv*
in**gre**dient *n*	**pal**let *n*	fit *adj*
layer *n*	**pro**duct sheet *n*	**lead**er *n*
liqueur *n*	**shelf**-life *n*	neat *adj*
liquid *n*	**stor**age *n*	**sci**ence *n*
mixture *n*	**JOBS**	**tech**nical *adj*
mould *n*	as**sem**bler *n*	**time**keeping *n*
pour *v*	ma**chine** operator *n*	
recipe *n*	**pack**er *n*	
shell *n*	**qual**ity control *n*	
tray *n*	**store**man *n*	

Grammar backup 7

The passive: present perfect passive

Practice

1 Look at the pictures which show how hamburgers are made. Complete the description using present and present perfect passive verb forms.

a First the meat and onion *are put* (put) in a bowl.
b Then they ..... (mix) together and an egg and seasoning ..... (add).
c After the mixture ..... (season), it ..... (roll) into small balls.
d Next the mixture ..... (place) in the fridge to cool.
e When the correct temperature ..... (reach), the hamburgers ..... (grill) on both sides.
f Finally, the hamburgers ..... (serve) with chips and salad.

2 Rewrite these sentences. Decide if you need to mention who performs the action.

a All over the world, people make thousands of phone calls every day.
   All over the world, thousands of phone calls are made every day.
b My secretary has already booked the ticket for you.
   Your ticket ..... .
c After they have checked the report, they send it to their customers.
   After the report ..... .
d Does the accounts department always pay the bills?
   Are ..... ?
e The bank hasn't found the documents I sent them.
   The documents ..... .
f The new cleaner has broken a glass table and two mugs.
   A glass table and two mugs ..... .

Reference

- We use passive structures to talk about what happens to people or things. They are often used in news reports or to describe processes when an impersonal style is important. Often the person who performs the action is unimportant, unknown or obvious: *The post **was delivered** at 8.30* (obviously by the postman). *His passport **has been stolen*** (and we don't know who stole it). *The chocolate **is heated** until it becomes liquid* (but it is unimportant who does it).

- The passive is formed with the appropriate tense of *be* + past participle. We use *by* if we want to mention the person or thing that performs the action: *The meeting **will be attended by** all the sales staff. The company **is being bought by** a Swiss bank.*

- The present perfect passive is often used to sequence two actions. It describes the action which happens first: *After the faxes **have been typed**, they are checked. The chocolates are packed into boxes when they **have been wrapped**.*

3 Translation

Write these sentences in your own language. Then close your Course Book. Translate the sentences back into English.

a Portuguese is spoken in Brazil.
b The office hasn't been redecorated for a long time.
c After the goods have been checked, they are delivered to the customer.

Adverbs

Practice

1 Choose the correct word.

a She types very ~~quick~~ / quickly.
b The meeting started late / lately because of the fire alarm.
c He works very hard / hardly.
d How are you? Very good / well, thank you.
e It's a good idea to drive slow / slowly. There are always a lot of accidents here.
f We've had a lot of orders from Japan lately / late.
g They've been good / well friends since they were children.

2 Rewrite these sentences.

a You work very efficiently.
  You're very efficient.
b She's a fast typist.
  She types ..... .
c He cooks well.
  He's a ..... .
d They take a long time to do their work.
  They work ..... .
e He has a very quiet voice.
  He speaks ..... .

3 Complete the sentences about yourself with a suitable adjective or adverb.

a I speak English ..... .
b I'm a ..... traveller.
c I usually arrive ..... for appointments.
d I'm a ..... student.

4 Translation

Write these sentences in your own language. Then close your Course Book. Translate the sentences back into English.

a I'm a good leader.
b I work well with my colleagues.
c I like working independently.

Reference

- We use adverbs of manner to describe how we do something. They describe a verb: *I always* **listen carefully** *to my teacher. My secretary* **types accurately**.

- Regular adverbs are formed by adding *-ly* to the adjective: *She's a* **careful** *driver. She drives* **carefully**.

- Adverbs of manner usually go directly after the verb or after the verb + noun: *They work* **independently**. *They solve problems* **calmly**.

- *Late*, *hard* and *fast* are used as adjectives and adverbs: *He's a* **hard** *worker; he works* **hard**. *I like* **fast** *cars; I drive* **fast**. *I've got a* **late** *appointment; I often work* **late**.

- *Lately* is not an adverb of manner – it means 'recently': *I haven't seen them* **lately**.

- *Hardly* means 'almost not'. It comes before a main verb or after an auxiliary: *I* **hardly** *spoke.* (I said very little.) *He can* **hardly** *speak any French.* (He speaks almost no French.)

- *Good* is an adjective; *well* is usually an adverb: *They're* **good** *workers. They work* **well**. We can also use *well* as an adjective to refer to health: *I'm* **well**.

Manufacturing Exporting

8

- Listen to an interview
- Describe tasks
- Listen to a job description
- Describe continuing change
- Write a fax
- Vocabulary:
  exporting
- Grammar:
  have something *done*

Action A — Dealing with export queries

Vocabulary: exporting

1 Look at this list of words connected with exporting. Group them under the headings below. Use a dictionary to help you.

| deliver | despatch | client | query | contact | fax | speak to |
| discuss | transport | problem | ship | buyer | fax | inquiry |

- To send   • To communicate   • A customer   • A question

Speaking and Listening: a job description

2 Imagine that you work as assistant to the export manager of a manufacturing company. What tasks do you think are involved in the job? Make a list. Use words from Exercise 1.

EXAMPLE: *Send order forms to clients.*

3 Karin Thielemans assists the Export Manager at Neuhaus. Listen. Which of these tasks does she do? Compare what she says with your list from Exercise 2.

a She handles queries from clients.
b She makes contact with new clients.
c She passes orders to the despatch department.
d She also gives them to the production manager.
e She sends out invoices.
f She arranges transportation for the products.
g She sends the client information about transport arrangements.

4 Listen to the last part of the interview again.

a Which of these areas does Karin deal with herself?

| United States | United Kingdom | Japan | Europe |
| Russia | South America | Middle East | Far East |

b What does the expression *everything from A to Z* mean?
c What is the effect of using *better and better* instead of just *better* in this sentence?
That's working better and better now.

Phrasebook

Describing continuing change

We're selling **more and more**.
Costs are getting **higher and higher**.
North Africa is becoming **less and less important**.
Finding good staff is **more and more difficult**.

62

Speaking: describing continuing change

5 Look at the *Phrasebook* on page 62.

a Change the expressions in bold to make sentences with the opposite meaning.

b Use similar expressions to complete the sentences below.
- I'm working ..... every year.
- The price of oil is getting ..... each year.
- My English is getting ..... .
- The market for luxury chocolates is getting ..... .
- The dollar is becoming ..... against our currency.

Grammar: *have* something *done*

6 Read the fax extract below.

a Who do you think it is from?
b Who do you think it is to?
c What is the writer going to do personally?
d What is someone else going to do? How do you know?
e Write the fax that this is a reply to.

Thank you for your fax requesting information about our products.

I am sending you the documentation by courier today. I will also speak to the Production Department and have a sample pack sent to you by air as soon as possible.

Yours sincerely

---

7 Make sentences with the correct form of *have* something *done*.

a I'm going to / some samples (send)
I'm going to have some samples sent.

b They're / new brochures (print)
c They are going to / a new house (build)
d The company will / some heaters (install)
e We're / the machines (repair)
f She has / her car (clean)

▶▶ p.68 **Grammar backup 8**

8 Work in pairs and look at the picture. You have taken office space in an old building for your new company. What do you plan to do? Decide what you will do yourselves and what you will ask someone else to do. Use these verbs to help you:

| paint | clean | deliver | buy | put | install |
| design | print | advertise | employ | write | |

EXAMPLE: *We'll buy some filing cabinets.*
We'll have some business cards printed.

Writing a fax

9 You work in an export department. You have received this fax and written notes on it. Write a fax reply telling the client what you and the other departments are going to do. Use words from Exercise 1.

One of our buyers visited your stand at the London Exhibition last week. He had a brief discussion with your Marketing Manager and we would now like to make further inquiries about your full product range.

Could you please send me the following as soon as possible:

1 A catalogue and current price list of all your export products; *me*

2 A copy of your most recent company report; *finance dept*

3 Any sample products that are available. *production dept*

We would also like one of your representatives to visit us here. Could you ask your sales manager to contact me to discuss this? *sales manager*

I look forward to hearing from you.

Yours faithfully

Manufacturing

Action B

- Read about franchises
- Make hypothetical statements
- Vocabulary:
  franchise businesses
  nouns ending in -ee/-er
- Grammar:
  second conditional sentences

Franchise businesses

Speaking and Reading: franchises

1 Neuhaus' parent company, Neuhaus-Mondose, has a number of franchise arrangements. For example, it owns most of the shares in Jeff de Bruges, a French chain of chocolate shops, and all of Jeff de Bruges International. Other companies with franchise arrangements include The Body Shop. Discuss these questions about franchise businesses in general.

a What is a franchise?

b Which of these are important features of a franchise business?
   - All the shops look exactly the same.
   - The products that they sell are identical.
   - Products cost the same.
   - All stock is bought from the parent company.
   - All advertising is done locally.

c Name other franchise businesses. What do they sell?

d What are the advantages and disadvantages of buying a franchise:
   - to the buyer?
   - to the parent company?

Reading about franchise businesses

2 Read about another company and check your answers to the questions in Exercise 1.

> When a company sells a franchise, it's really selling its reputation. So a successful company can sell a licence for someone to use its name in a particular area – perhaps in the same country as the parent company or, often, in another country. In return, the shop sells the company's products and gives the company a share of its profits. If you want to buy a Kids' World franchise, for example, you'll have to pay between £50,000 and £100,000 – it depends on the size of the shop. This gives you the name, an exclusive geographical area, the design of the shop and the packaging, shop fittings, staff uniforms and full training for all personnel. All stock is bought from us and no other products can be sold. We also take a percentage of the profits. One of our duties is to support our network of franchise shops by advertising internationally and running regular promotional campaigns. If a franchisee has a problem, we'll help and advise them. But we'd certainly close a shop if a franchisee's behaviour damaged the company's good name.

64

3 Find these words in the text. Then match them with definitions a – i below.

reputation	share	licence	fittings
personnel	support	network	exclusive
damage			

a a group of shops
b a part of the profits
c official written permission for a company to do something
d for one company's use only
e furniture and equipment in a workplace
f other people's opinion of a company
g to hurt
h people who work for a company
i to help

Vocabulary: nouns ending in -ee/-er

4 Answer the questions.

a Find *franchisee* in the text. Which of these does it refer to?
 • The company that *buys* the right to run the shop?
 • The company that *sells* the right to run the shop?

b Now look at these pairs of words. Which ending (*-ee/-er*) is used to describe:
 • the person who *performs* the action (training, employing, interviewing)?
 • the person who the action *is done to*?

| trainee – trainer | interviewee – interviewer |
| employee – employer | |

c So what do you think these words mean?

| addressee | licensee | payee |

Talking point

"I HATE ALL THESE CHAINS OF SHOPS AND RESTAURANTS. SOON CITIES WILL ALL LOOK EXACTLY THE SAME."

What do *you* think?

Grammar: second conditional sentences

5 Compare these two sentences from the text.

 A First conditional: *If a franchisee has a problem, we'll help and advise them.*
 B Second conditional: *We'd certainly close a shop if a franchisee's behaviour damaged the company's good name.*

a The situations in the *if* clauses are both possible, but one is more likely (and so more real) than the other. Which one?
b Which verb forms are used in the *if* clauses?
c Which verb forms are used in the other clauses? What are the full forms of *we'll* and *we'd*?
d So when do we use a second conditional sentence? How do we form one?

6 Work in pairs. Decide which situations below are more or less likely. Write first or second conditional sentences to show the effect of each situation.

 EXAMPLE: make a large profit in the company's first year
 If the company made a large profit in the first year, we would double the number of staff.

a increase the prices of products slightly
b double staff salaries
c send the parcel by sea
d let all the staff go on holiday at the same time
e not receive a share of the profits from a franchisee

7 Discuss what *you* would do. Complete the sentences.

a If I had enough money to start a company, I'd ..... .
b If I could live in any country, I'd ..... .
c I'd ..... if I could choose any job that I wanted.
d I'd ..... if I could buy a franchise.

▶▶ p69 Grammar backup 8

Manufacturing

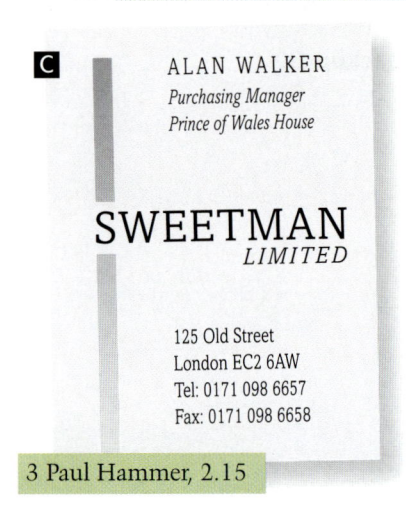

Action C — Assisting callers

- Describe a receptionist's duties
- Receive a visitor
- Understand and take messages
- Say no politely
- Vocabulary:
  reception duties

Speaking: reception duties

1 Eliane van Laethem is a receptionist and secretary at the Neuhaus headquarters. List the activities you think she does. Use these verbs and nouns to help you.

EXAMPLE: *She greets visitors.*

VERBS		NOUNS	
greet	receive	appointments	diary
welcome	put through	meetings	telephone calls
make	arrange	faxes	visitors
take	give	letters	directions
send	keep	courier packages	
help		messages	

A

Devon
IMPORTS

Sarah Thelman
INTERNATIONAL RELATIONS

Devon Imports Ltd
51 Ship Street
Exeter EX34 2OM
Tel: 01392 345123
Fax: 01392 345990

1 Robert Daniels 10.00

B

Richard Hansen
Sales Executive

BAXTER SHIPPING

Transport House
Station Industrial Estate
Southampton SO12 1RD
Tel: 01703 562348
Fax: 01703 562539

2 Karin Thielemans, 11.30

C

ALAN WALKER
Purchasing Manager
Prince of Wales House

SWEETMAN
LIMITED

125 Old Street
London EC2 6AW
Tel: 0171 098 6657
Fax: 0171 098 6658

3 Paul Hammer, 2.15

Listening and Speaking: receiving a visitor

2 Listen to the conversation and answer the questions.
a Who does the visitor want to see?
b What time is his / her appointment?
c Which of the business cards belongs to the visitor?

3 Write the visitor's part of the conversation.

Visitor: Hello.
Receptionist: Good morning. Can I help you?
Visitor: ..... .
Receptionist: I see. Could I take your name?
Visitor: ..... .
Receptionist: And which company are you from, Mr Walker?
Visitor: ..... .
Receptionist: Sweetman?
Visitor: ..... .
Receptionist: Right. Just a moment, please. I'll call her... She'll be down in a few minutes, Mr Walker. Would you like to take a seat?
Visitor: ..... .

4 Work in pairs. Use the *Phrasebook* below to help you.

A: You are a visitor. Choose one of the business cards on page 66 and speak to a receptionist.
B: Take the part of the receptionist.

Now change roles.

Phrasebook

Receiving a visitor

Can I help you?
Could I take your name, please?
Could you tell me your name?
Which company are you from?
Could you tell me the name of your company, please?
Just a moment. I'll tell her you're here.
I'll see if she's free.
She'll be here in a moment.
Would you like to take a seat?
Can I get you something to drink?
Can I take your coat?

Listening and Reading: telephone messages

5 Listen to three telephone conversations with a receptionist. Match the phone calls to the messages, A – C below, that the receptionist wrote.

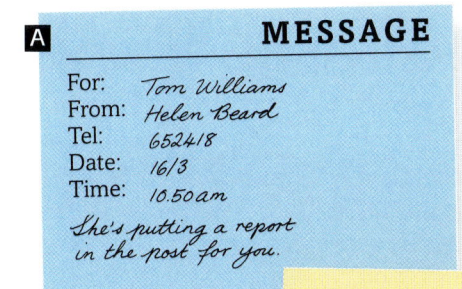

A MESSAGE
For: Tom Williams
From: Helen Beard
Tel: 652418
Date: 16/3
Time: 10.50 am
She's putting a report in the post for you.

B MESSAGE
For: Peter Allen
From: Mrs Allen
Tel:
Date: 16/3
Time: 11.05 am
Please call your wife at home.

C MESSAGE
For: Jennifer Street
From: John Locker
Tel:
Date: 16/3
Time: 11.45 am
Can you meet him after work?

6 Now listen to the three conversations again. Add any important information that is missing from the messages.

Speaking: saying *no* politely

7 Look at these four sentences. Why are the sentences on the right more polite?

- She can't see you.
- I'm afraid she can't see you right now. She's in a meeting.

- I have to cancel our meeting.
- I'm afraid I have to cancel our meeting. My son's having an operation and I need to be with him.

8 Reply politely in these situations. Explain why it is not possible to help.

a A visitor wants to see Ms Thielemans but she's away.
b A driver arrives with a courier package but he has come to the wrong building.
c A visitor asks if he can smoke.
d A visitor wants to visit the factory shop. It is closed until tomorrow.
e A visitor wants to make a personal international phone call from your phone.

Word file Unit 8

PEOPLE
addres**see** n
client n
employ**ee** n
intervie**wee** n
licen**see** n
pay**ee** n
person**nel** n
pro**duc**tion manager n
purchasing manager n
sales executive n
train**ee** n

FRANCHISES
ex**clu**sive adj
fittings n pl
franchi**see** n
licence n
network n
share n
sup**port** v

OTHER WORDS
cancel v
company re**port** n
con**tact** n/v
deal with v

documen**ta**tion n
in**qui**ry n
in**stall** v
price list n
product range n
query n
repu**ta**tion n

Grammar backup 8

Have something done

Practice

1 Write a sentence for each picture.

a he / computer / deliver / tomorrow
He is having the computer delivered tomorrow.

b she / suit / clean / yesterday
She ..... .

c they / just / the photocopier / repaired
They ..... .

d I / the tyres / check / every six months
I ..... .

e you / the book cover / design / last week?
Did ..... ?

f we / our office / redecorated / at the moment
We ..... .

2 Which of the things below:

a do you often have done?
b have you had done in the past six months?
c did you have done last year?
d are you going to have done?

machines repaired	clothes dry-cleaned
letters / reports typed	faxes sent	hair cut
room redecorated	name cards printed
passport stamped	photos developed
shoes mended	eyes tested	teeth checked

EXAMPLE: *I have my hair cut every month.*

3 Translation

Write these sentences in your own language. Then close your Course Book. Translate the sentences back into English.

a I have my car serviced every six months.
b She is going to have some flowers sent to Lucy.
c He didn't have his post forwarded.

Reference

- We use *have* something *done* when something is done for us by someone else, often as a professional service. The structure has a passive meaning: *I'm going to* **have my house renovated** *(by a builder)*. *They've* **had the figures checked** *(by the accountant)*.
- The structure can be used with different tenses:

I	have	my car	washed once a week.
He	is having	his office	repainted at the moment.
She	had	the report	faxed to her office.
We	are going to have	central heating	installed next week.
You	have had	your hair	cut.
They	will have	their passport photos	taken tomorrow.

- We can use *get* instead of *have*. *Get* is more informal: *I* **got / had** *the invitations printed.*

68

Second conditional

Practice

1 Match the halves of the sentences a – e with 1 – 6.

a If I were you,
b We'll move house
c We'd move house
d If sales don't increase
e If the company decided to move,
f It'll be much better

1 if I get a pay rise.
2 the situation will be serious.
3 I'd ask Silvia.
4 it would be very inconvenient for me.
5 if you phone the bank now.
6 if Roger got a pay rise.

2 Complete the sentences.

a If I were the managing director of Coca Cola, ...
b I wouldn't always be so tired if ..... .
c It'll be easy to get promotion if ..... .
d If the company does well this year, ...

3 Correct the mistakes.

a If you left home earlier, you ~~won't~~ *wouldn't* be late for work.
b If it won't rain this afternoon, I'll go for a walk.
c She would get the job if she would speak better English.
d If they will invite me, I'll go with them.
e They'd get more work done if they was more efficient.
f If I were you, I'll fly first class.
g What do you do if you won a lot of money?

4 Translation

Write these sentences in your own language. Then close your Course Book. Translate the sentences back into English.

a If they offered me a job in the States, I'd take it.
b If they give me a rise, I'll buy a new car.
c What would you do if you were in my place?

Reference

- We use the second conditional to talk about the result of an unlikely or impossible situation in the present or future: *If people **stopped** eating chocolate, the company **would go** bankrupt. If Peter **didn't smoke**, h**e'd be** much healthier. What **would** you **do** if you won a lot of money?*

- We use the first conditional instead of the second conditional if we think the situation is more likely. Compare:
*If I **have** the time, I**'ll go** shopping.* (You will probably have the time.)
*If I **had** the time, I**'d go** shopping.* (You don't have the time.)
*If I **have** enough money, I**'ll buy** the company.* (Said by a millionaire.)
*If I **had** enough money, I**'d buy** the company.* (Said by an employee.)

- There are two parts to a conditional sentence. The *if* clause can come before or after the main clause: *If sales increased, the company would make a large profit. The company would make a large profit if sales increased.*

- After *I* and *he*, we often use *were*: *If I **were** rich, I'd buy a large house.* However, it is more common to use *was* in spoken English: *If I **was** rich, I'd buy a large house.*

- The expression *If I were you* is used to give advice: ***If I were you**, I'd go to the doctor.*

Media
On screen

9

Action A

- Read the results of a survey
- Discuss programme types
- Understand and describe preferences
- Read and write a viewer profile
- Vocabulary:
   programme types
   compounds with *well-* and *badly-*

Viewing

Vocabulary: programme types

1 The New World Youth Study asked young people in 26 countries about their television viewing preferences. Look at the results.

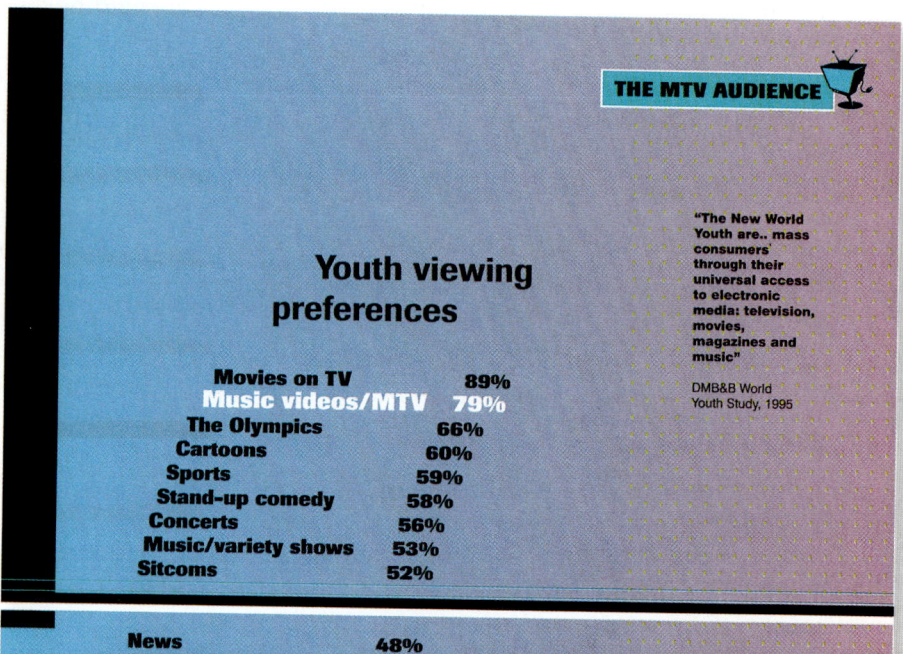

THE MTV AUDIENCE

Youth viewing preferences

Movies on TV	89%
Music videos/MTV	79%
The Olympics	66%
Cartoons	60%
Sports	59%
Stand-up comedy	58%
Concerts	56%
Music/variety shows	53%
Sitcoms	52%
News	48%
Academy awards	47%
Talk shows	43%
Game shows	42%
Dramas	35%
Soap Operas	33%

Source: DMB&B World Youth Study 1995

"The New World Youth are.. mass consumers through their universal access to electronic media: television, movies, magazines and music"

DMB&B World Youth Study, 1995

a Find programmes in the survey in which:
   • the best actors are given prizes
   • a comedian performs in front of a live audience
   • there are a lot of different types of entertainment
   • ordinary people play games for prizes
   • the day's events are reported
   • a comedy programme is based on a particular situation

b Which programme types are shown in the pictures?

c Name particular programmes from television in your own country that are examples of each type.

EXAMPLE: *'EastEnders' is a soap opera. It is set in the East End of London, and dramatic events happen to ordinary people.*

70

Listening and Speaking: describing preferences

2 Listen to a group of people talking about their television viewing habits. Complete the chart.

	LIKES	DISLIKES
A	concerts, music videos	game shows
B	.....	.....
C	.....	.....
D	.....	.....
E	.....	.....

3 Work in pairs. Discuss your own viewing preferences, and give reasons for them. Use expressions from the *Phrasebook* to help you.

Phrasebook

Describing preferences

I prefer watching concerts.
I prefer comedy programmes **to** game shows. They're **the best**.
I like stand-up comedy **better than** sitcoms.
I'd rather watch a film than a talk show.
I can't stand / can't bear talk shows.
My favourite / least favourite programmes are movies.
I watch cartoons **a lot**.
I never watch sitcoms.
I'm interested in drama.

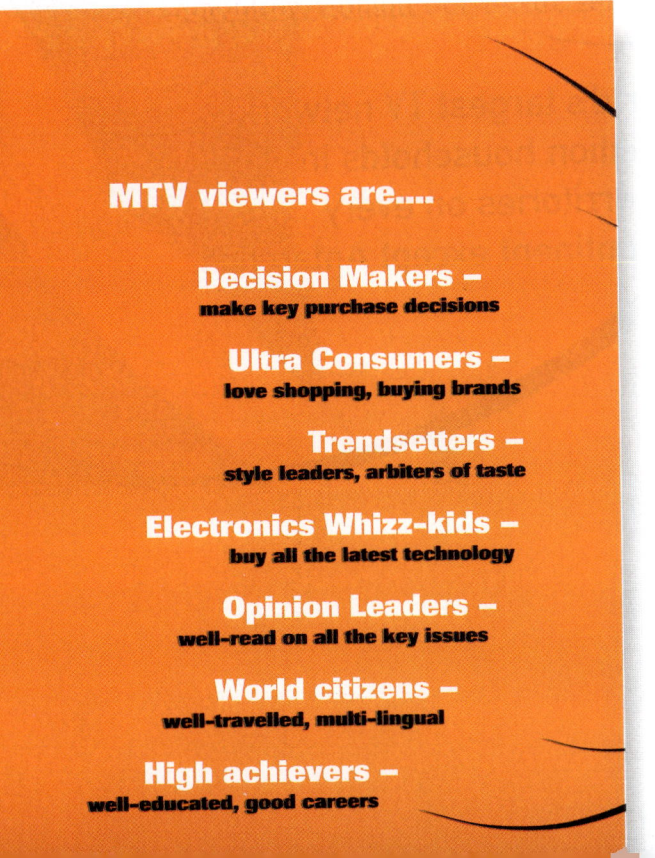

MTV viewers are....

Decision Makers – make key purchase decisions

Ultra Consumers – love shopping, buying brands

Trendsetters – style leaders, arbiters of taste

Electronics Whizz-kids – buy all the latest technology

Opinion Leaders – well-read on all the key issues

World citizens – well-travelled, multi-lingual

High achievers – well-educated, good careers

Reading: a viewer profile

4 Read the text about MTV viewers and answer the questions. Use a dictionary to help you.

a Why is it important, do you think, for a television company to know its audience? How can this information help the company?

b Find phrases that describe:
 • what MTV viewers do • what MTV viewers are

c Which of these products do you think would interest MTV viewers? Why?

CDs   travel books   financial products
sports goods   children's toys
fashion magazines   educational books
computer games   family cars   furniture
office equipment   Internet software

d Which of these words describe a typical MTV viewer, according to the text? Explain your choices.

modern   old-fashioned   young   lazy
middle-aged   independent   intelligent
thoughtful   poor   wealthy   fashionable
open-minded   well-educated

Vocabulary: compounds with *well-* / *badly-*

5 Find compound words in the text that begin with *well-*.

a What part of speech follows *well-*?

b Rewrite these sentences using new compounds that begin with *well-* or *badly-*.

EXAMPLE: *I like the design of the building.*
The building's well-designed.

• She didn't plan the reception well.
 The reception ...
• There are a lot of mistakes in this letter.
 This letter ...
• He is wearing very smart clothes. *He is ...*
• The reps didn't promote the product properly.
 The product ...

Speaking and Writing: a viewer profile

6 Work in pairs. Think of another TV station that you know – a specialist one (e.g. CNN, Eurosport) or an ordinary national one. Make a list like the MTV profile on the left.

EXAMPLE: *CNN viewers are ... international business people – well-travelled, with good careers.*

Media

Action B **MTV Europe**

- Talk and read about a company
- Listen for main points
- Rephrasing
- Read and write slogans

"Think globally, act locally"
Marshall McLuhan, The Medium is the Message

MTV: A GLOBAL BRAND

1 in every 4 households in the world receives MTV

MTV US 62.6 million
MTV Europe 54 million
MTV Brasil 14.1 million
MTV Mandarin 12.3 million
MTV Asia 11.6 million
MTV Latino 6.7 million
MTV Japan 1.2 million
Syndicated networks 104 million worldwide

The world's largest TV network – 266 million households in 75 territories on every continent except Antarctica.

The Smashing Pumpkins at the MTV Europe Music Awards

Speaking and reading about a company

1 What do you know, or what can you guess about MTV?

a What types of programme is it known for?

b What is the main age range of
- MTV viewers?   • MTV presenters?

c How do people receive MTV in your country?
- by satellite?   • by cable?
- via normal TV channels?

2 Look at the photograph and text opposite.

a MTV is described as a *global brand*. What does this mean? Use a dictionary to help you, if necessary.

b One of MTV's slogans is *Think globally, act locally*. In what ways do you think MTV tries to be global and at the same time to have local interest?

c How many households are there in the world, according to the text? So what is a *household*?

d What do you think is meant by
- *territories*?   • *syndicated networks*?

Listening for main points

3 You are going to listen to an interview with Iain Renwick, Vice President of Communications at MTV Europe. Do you think these statements are true or false?

a All MTV programmes are in English.

b Each MTV programme is shown all over the world.

Listen and check your answers. Correct the false statements. What information can you add?

Reading and Speaking: rephrasing

4 Rewrite these interview extracts in simpler language. Use a dictionary to help you.

EXAMPLE: *The international language of music is predominantly English.*
Most international performers sing in English.

a The content of the channels across the world is driven by the needs of the local markets.

b In south-east Asia we're going language-specific.

c There's obviously a lot of programming that covers all our channels.

d One cannot deliver solely with one message for Europe.

5 Look at the sentences in Exercise 4 again. Rephrase them orally to make the language simpler. Use expressions from the *Phrasebook*.

EXAMPLE: *The international language of music is predominantly English.*

What I mean is that most international performers sing in English.

Phrasebook

Rephrasing

In other words, it's great.
What I mean is that I really like it.
To put it another way, it appeals to me a lot.
I mean, it's my kind of TV station.
That is, it interests me.

6 Work in pairs.

A: Describe the plot of a film or television programme that you have seen recently. Explain why it interested you. Rephrase if your partner does not understand.

B: Your partner is going to tell you about a film or television programme. If you do not understand, ask him / her to rephrase. Say: *Sorry?* or *What do you mean?*

Reading and Writing: slogans

7 Remember the MTV slogan. How appropriate does it now seem to you? Read the advertising slogans below.

a What do they mean?

b What do they tell you about the product?

- ‘Be good. Be bad. Just Be.’
  (Calvin Klein's 'Be' perfume)

- ‘All men are created equal.
  All cars are not.’
  (Honda cars)

- ‘See. Hear. Feel.’
  (Bang & Olufsen sound systems)

c What slogans do you remember from advertisements? Why do you remember them?

d Work in groups. Choose a company or a product and write a slogan for it. Compare your slogan with other students'. Which is the best?

Media

Action C | **Special events**

- Talk about events
- Read and write a letter
- Vocabulary: reporting verbs
- Grammar: reported speech

Speaking: special events

1 Look at the pictures below.

a Who are the people in the pictures?
b What kind of event are they attending?
c Have you ever seen an event like this?
d What similar events take place for people with other jobs?
e What do you expect the presenter to say at the events below?
f What do you expect the people in the pictures to say?

Grammar: reported speech

2 Look at these extracts from written reports of an Awards Ceremony.

a Underline the reporting verb in each sentence.
   EXAMPLE: *The presenter <u>announced</u> that the company was giving a special award.*
   - She said that the award was for the best new band.
   - She asked the band when they would make their next album.
   - The singer replied that they had just finished one.
   - He added that the band were going to tour Europe in the summer.
   - The presenter asked if they enjoyed touring.
   - The band explained that they would like to tour as much as possible.
   - The singer told the audience that they were honoured to receive the award. But he said they could not accept it.

b Do you know any other reporting verbs?

3 Look at the sentences in Exercise 2 again.

a Which ones report
   - statements?   - questions?

b Which reporting verb is always followed by an object?

c Which sentences report the ones below? What changes were made?
   - 'The company is giving a special award.'   - 'We've just finished one.'
   - 'Do you enjoy touring?'

d Write the speakers' actual words, reported in the other sentences in Exercise 2.

e Complete the chart. Which form does not change when it is reported?

Direct speech	Reported speech
is giving	was giving
.....	was
.....	would make
.....	had just finished
.....	were going to tour
.....	enjoyed
.....	would like to tour
.....	were honoured
.....	could not accept

▶▶ p.76 **Grammar backup 9**

74

Unit **9C**

Reading and Writing: a letter

4 Read the letter on the right and then look at the pictures below. What problems did the *Motel Lizards* find at the hotel?

I'm afraid your rooms aren't ready yet.

Here's the car you ordered.

Chicken, sir?

Your bill comes to £475. How would you like to pay?

The Manager
Queen's Bridge Hotel
Liverpool

April 16th

Dear Mr Edmunds

Following our telephone conversation of earlier today.

I am writing to confirm the arrangements for the *Motel Lizards*.

Dates:	May 25 – 27
Rooms:	5 doubles
Arrival time:	11 a.m.
Food:	Vegetarian lunches on 25th and 26th
Transport:	A 12-seater minibus plus driver available for the whole period
Payment:	Invoice MCA International

Yours sincerely

Jem Stephens

Jem Stephens
Human Resources, MCA

5 You are Jem Stephens. The *Motel Lizards* have just left. Write to the hotel and complain about the problems. Start your letter like this:

I am writing to complain about ...
When we discussed the arrangements on the phone, I explained that ...

Word file Unit 9

TELEVISION
cable *n*
channel *n*
entertainment *n*
global *adj*
satellite *n*
view *n*
viewer *n*

PROGRAMMES
award *n*
cartoon *n*
ceremony *n*
comedy *n*
concert *n*
drama *n*
game show *n*
movie *n*
news *n*
sitcom *n*
soap opera *n*
talk show *n*
variety show *n*

PEOPLE
comedian *n*
consumer *n*
decision-maker *n*
fashionable *adj*
independent *adj*
lazy *adj*
multi-lingual *adj*
old-fashioned *adj*
open-minded *adj*
thoughtful *adj*
trend setter *n*
vegetarian *n/adj*
wealthy *adj*
well-educated *adj*
well-travelled *adj*
whizz-kid *n*

REPORTING VERBS
add *v*
announce *v*
complain *v*
reply *v*

OTHER WORDS
brand *n*
can't bear *v*
can't stand *v*
cultural diversity *n*
favourite *adj*
household *n*
key issue *n*
slogan *n*
style *n*
survey *n*
taste *n*
territory *n*
would rather *v*

Grammar backup 9

Reported speech

Practice

1 Report these sentences.

a I often go to bed late.
She said that she often went to bed late.

b Did you watch the awards ceremony last night?
He asked me ..... .

c They've never been stopped in a security check here before.
She told me ..... .

d We're going to install satellite television tomorrow.
He said that ..... .

e Can you contact me about the franchise later?
She asked us ..... .

f If we don't leave soon, we'll be late again.
I told them ..... .

2 Translation

Write these sentences in your own language. Then close your Course Book. Translate the sentences back into English.

a 'We've written to you three times.' They said that they had written to us three times.

b 'Were you at work yesterday?' He asked me if I had been at work the day before.

c 'How often do you have departmental meetings?' They asked us how often we had departmental meetings.

d 'Don't phone after 10 o'clock.' I told him not to phone after 10 o'clock.

Reference

- We often have to make changes when reporting sentences and questions, especially to verb tenses.

DIRECT SPEECH	REPORTED SPEECH
Present tenses	**Past tenses**
'We **enjoy** being here.'	They said they **enjoyed** being there.
'I**'m learning** to drive.'	She announced that she **was learning** to drive.
'I**'ve** already **seen** this film.'	He told me that he **had** already **seen** the film.
Past tense	**Past tense**
'She **met** them yesterday.'	He explained that she **met** (**had met**) them the day before.

- Present forms of modal verbs (*can, may, shall, will, must*) often change to past forms (*could, might, should, would, had to*): 'We **will** see you later.' They said they **would** see me later. Past forms do not change.

- If a statement is still true we do not need to change the tense: *He said he's ill.* (He said this very recently.)

- Clearly, pronouns and references to times and places, like *here* and *today*, often change in reports.

- Questions are reported using *if*, *whether* or a question word; we use the word order of a statement: *He asked **if we had met** before. She asked me **when I was leaving**.*

- Unlike other reporting verbs, *tell* is always followed by an object: *They **told us** that it was lunchtime. Ask* can also be followed by an object.

- *Ask* and *tell* are followed by an object and an infinitive in reported requests and orders: *She asked / told **us to be** quiet.*

76

Sound check

Running words together

Words ending in *t* or *d*

1. **When a word ends in *t* or *d* and these letters come between two consonants, they are often not pronounced.**

   a Practise saying these words on their own. Then listen and check.

   > sound   frequent   lost   must

   b Now listen to these expressions. Notice what happens to the *t* and *d* underlined.

   > soun<u>d s</u>ystem   frequen<u>t f</u>lyer   los<u>t l</u>uggage
   > you mus<u>t b</u>e Jill

   c Practise saying these expressions. Then listen and repeat.

   > product range   department store
   > trend setter   hand-made

2. **The *t* or *d* sound at the end of a word often disappears when followed by a word beginning with *p* or *b*.**

   a Listen to these expressions. Then listen again and repeat.

   > chocola<u>te b</u>ar   gui<u>de</u>book   goo<u>d b</u>oy
   > mea<u>t p</u>acker   tha<u>t p</u>assenger

   b Practise saying these sentences. Then listen and check.
   - I'd been there before.
   - It's a hand-made product.
   - She's quite poor.

Words ending in *n*

1. **When a word ends in *n* and the following word begins with *p* or *b*, the final *n* sounds more like *m*.**

   a Listen to these sentences. Then listen again and repeat.
   - Eleve<u>n p</u>eople are waiting.
   - There's only o<u>ne p</u>assenger.
   - I ca<u>n b</u>e there at five.
   - I'll see you at the statio<u>n b</u>ookshop.

   b Practise saying these sentences. Then listen and check.
   - Ten passengers have missed the flight.
   - He's still in bed.
   - She's away on business.
   - There's one picture left.

2. **When a word ends in *n* and is followed by a word beginning with *c* or *g*, the *n* is often pronounced like *ng*.**

   a Listen to these sentences. Then listen again and repeat.
   - One pallet holds ni<u>ne c</u>artons.
   - He's an America<u>n c</u>lient.
   - I've got a brow<u>n c</u>oat.
   - We ca<u>n g</u>o tomorrow.

   b Practise saying these sentences. Then listen and check.
   - Neuhaus is a Belgian confectioner.
   - Please go to the green car park.
   - He can get it.
   - I've got an Australian guidebook.

Media

Market research

10

Action A — Consumers

- Read about market research
- Write questions
- Carry out market research
- Vocabulary and Grammar: phrasal verbs

Reading market research

1 **Imagine you are the marketing manager of a company that manufactures one of the products below.**

a What information would you like from consumers?
b How can all this information be collected?

2 **Companies often hire a market research agency to gather information for them. Put these steps in the order you think they happen.**

a Specialist staff interview people.
b A client brings a problem to a market research agency.
c The client agrees to the plan.
d The agency puts together a market research plan.
e The questionnaire information is entered into a computer.
f The data is analysed.
g The agency plans the interviews.
h Main research findings are presented to the client.

78

Unit 10A

RESEARCHING THE MARKET

Companies *carry out* market research to *find out* what people think about their products or services. It is also valuable to know what potential consumers feel about social issues – what their attitudes and opinions are – as well as what they actually buy, read, listen to or watch. All this information is then used to create products and services that consumers actually want, and to select the most suitable media for advertising them. Most companies do some research themselves, but larger organisations often *take on* a research agency to collect the information they need.

Janice Hare is a director at Research Matters, a major international market research agency. Corporate clients bring problems to her. For example, they want to know why their competitors' products are more popular than their own. She decides on the type of people to interview and the questions to ask them. She may also decide where interviews should be conducted. Should they be done on the street or in people's homes? Is there a need to *set up* meetings in special interview rooms? Research Matters then *puts forward* a market research plan to the client for approval. When the client agrees to *go ahead*, the questionnaire *is drawn up* and specialist interviewing staff begin collecting the data.

Information recorded at the different interviews from each questionnaire is put into a computer and Janice's team then analyses the data to *find out* answers to whatever their clients want to know. They *put together* an easy-to-read report with charts and diagrams, summarising the main findings from the research. This is then presented to the client.

---

3 Read the text and answer these questions.

a Why are market researchers interested in what people read, listen to or watch?
b Who hires agencies like *Research Matters*?
c Check your answer to Exercise 2 opposite.

Vocabulary: phrasal verbs

4 Replace the underlined words in these sentences with the correct form of a phrasal verb (in italics) from the text.

a Companies want to discover what consumers want.
b A plan is prepared.
c Janice suggests a plan to the client.
d Interviews are done by special staff.
e Janice's PA arranges the interviews.
f They may need to employ new staff.
g The interviews can start.
h The report is assembled by the whole team.

Grammar: phrasal verbs

5 Phrasal verbs consist of a verb + adverb / preposition. Look again at the ones in the article.

a Do they all have an object? What is the object in each case?
b Look at the four sentences below. Why is the last sentence incorrect?
- They're setting a new project up.
- They're setting it up.
- They're setting up a new project.
- ~~They're setting up it.~~

6 Complete the sentences with the words in brackets. How many positions are there for these words?

a Would you like to try out? (this computer)
b If you've got a problem, can we talk over? (it)
c These papers come from my office. Can you please put back. (them)
d I'd like to put forward for the manager's job. (her)
e I'll need to contact you. Can I write down? (your phone number)

▶▶ p.84 **Grammar backup 10**

Writing and Speaking: market research

7 Work in pairs. Choose one of the products in Exercise 1.

a Write questions that a market research company might want to ask. You could, for example, ask about:
- personal details
- interests and spare time activities, including reading and viewing habits
- similar products that they use, know about or have seen advertisements for

b Now interview your partner.
A: Ask questions about the product. **B:** Give true answers.
Then change roles.
B: Ask and answer about one of the other products opposite, or a product that interests you. **A:** Answer your partner's questions.

Media

Action B **Keeping in touch**

- Discuss ways of getting feedback
- Read a press release
- Talk about information in a table
- Read and write about the results of a survey
- Compare and contrast
- Vocabulary: marketing words

Discussion: getting feedback

1 How can producers of TV and radio programmes and magazines interact with their audiences? Two examples are illustrated below. Discuss others.

BE ON TV!
Do you have a hobby that you love so much that it's taking over your life? If so, we'd like to hear from you. And there's a chance you'll appear on the new Channel 8 show ...
I just can't stop!

Reading a press release

2 Read the text below and answer the questions.
a Look at the headline. Who does the word *they* refer to?
b What were the two main purposes of the *Turned on Europe* project?
c C&A is a major retail clothing company. What part do you think it played in the project?
d What was the purpose of the MTV bus?
e What kinds of programmes appeared on MTV as a result of the project?
f In what ways do you think the project was useful to:
 • MTV? • C&A?

MTV Audience Research tells us who they are, what they buy and how they feel

MTV Europe has a continuing programme of events, promotions and campaigns that are directed at young people throughout Europe. A recent project that combined audience research with programme making was Turned on Europe. The project, a joint initiative of MTV and C&A, aimed to find out exactly how young Europeans live their lives by inviting them to film themselves and their friends discussing issues that affect them. A specially-equipped MTV bus travelled across Europe; it provided film-making facilities for young people who wanted to take part.

The survey itself involved face-to-face interviews with 1600 16–24 year olds from eight European countries – Germany, Holland, Poland, Sweden, France, Italy, Spain and Britain. It focused on attitudes and lifestyles and covered areas like: sex and marriage, attitudes to other Europeans, religion, immigration, racism and sexism, drugs, law and order, education, employment, the environment and politics. The result was a week of programmes on MTV. These featured many of the videos made during the project as well as a live phone-in discussion on some of the key issues. Another outcome was, of course, the survey results.

Vocabulary: marketing words

3 Match these words from the text with the definitions a – e.

event   promotion   campaign   project   survey

a an examination of people's behaviour or opinions
b something that happens that is important, interesting or unusual
c a plan to do something
d advertising, or a particular set of activities for advertising something
e business actions intended to obtain a particular result

Reading and Speaking: describing the results of a survey

4 Look at these results from the *Turned on Europe* survey.

a Are these statements true or false? Correct the false ones.
- Most people think school is a waste of time.
- Fewer Poles than Germans feel that good school results help them to get a job.
- A lot of French people believe that a degree is more useful now than it was.

b Work in pairs. A: Make statements about the table. B: Say whether your partner's statements are true or false. Then change roles.

	School is a waste of time	Doing well helps get a job	Degree less valuable than used to be
Average total	12%	71%	55%
UK	14%	80%	61%
Germany	13%	86%	51%
Holland	7%	81%	48%
Poland	20%	60%	32%
Sweden	10%	63%	43%
Spain	13%	82%	64%
France	17%	67%	77%
Italy	8%	54%	69%

5 Look at these survey extracts. Which parts of the table above do they describe?

> Few young people think that school is a waste of time, although only half feel that success helps to get a better job. The majority also believe that a university degree is less useful these days.

> Fifty-five per cent of young Europeans feel that degrees are less valuable than they used to be. The highest percentage of people with this view is in France (77%), and the percentage in Italy is only slightly lower. Young people in Poland are most positive about degrees. The Swedes, the Dutch and the Germans are also more positive than the average European, whereas in Spain and Britain a far higher percentage feel that degrees are less useful now.

Vocabulary: common words in survey reports

6 Look at the reports again. Find:
a three verbs for expressing opinions.
b two words that introduce contrasting information.
c words or phrases that mean:
- not many.
- most people.
- the largest number of people.
- a much larger number of people.

Writing: survey results

7 Work in pairs. Write statements about:
- Germany
- Poland
- Britain

Use the first report in Exercise 5 and the *Phrasebook* to help you.

Phrasebook

Comparing and contrasting

On the one hand, Italians believe in school education. **On the other hand**, many believe that a degree is unhelpful.
Although I went to university, I'm not sure it's the best thing for my son.
A very small percentage of young people in Britain speak a foreign language well, **whereas** most young Scandinavians speak a number of languages.
A higher percentage of young women speak foreign languages **than** young men.
Far more people go to university in the United States **than** in Europe.
Slightly fewer Dutch people think school is a waste of time **than** Italians.

---

8 Write a general paragraph describing the results of the question, *Do you think school is a waste of time?*

Media

Action C

Behind the scenes

- Talk about viewing figures
- Listen to an interview
- Interpret a chart
- Summarise information from a chart
- Vocabulary:
    audience research
    collective nouns
- Grammar:
    so / neither / nor

Speaking: viewing figures

1 Look at these viewing figures for one week of British television programmes.

a What do they show?
b Why do you think this information is useful to television companies?

WHAT THE NATION WATCHED

BBC1	MILLIONS	BBC2	MILLIONS	ITV	MILLIONS	C4	MILLIONS
EastEnders (Thu/Sun)	19.08	Red Dwarf	6.86	Coronation Street (Mon)	18.04	Brookside (Fri/Sat)	5.71
National Lottery Live (Sat)	11.45	Horizon	5.63	Emmerdale (Tue/Wed)	14.11	Countdown (Tue)	4.39
Neighbours (Tue)	10.94	Top Gear	5.24	Jane Eyre	12.52	ER	4.29
This is Your Life	10.34	Gardener's World	5.10	The Bill (Thu)	11.49	Last Chance Lottery	3.40
Crime Traveller	10.05	Food and Drink	4.20	Champions League Live	11.07	Hollyoaks (Thu/Sun)	3.05

Listening: an interview

2 Listen to Vanessa Sackarnd, a Programming Research Analyst at MTV. Answer the questions.

a Which country is she particularly interested in? Why?
b What information does she receive about that country?
c How does she use this information?
d Who else in MTV needs this information. Why?
e How does Vanessa's work help MTV to make programming decisions?

Vocabulary: audience research

3 Match these words with those underlined in sentences a – f. Use a dictionary to help you.

| data | target | time slot | plot | peaks | dips | scheduling |

a When she's got the information she uses it to draw a graph.
b A graph lets you see all the highs and lows.
c They have to know which audience they are going to aim at.
d More viewers watch MTV in the seven to nine o'clock period than any other.
e They sometimes change the timetabling of shows after feedback from viewers.

Vocabulary: collective nouns

4 Collective nouns refer to a group of people or things. We can often use them with a singular or a plural verb. The choice depends on whether we see the group as individuals or a single unit.

EXAMPLE: *Our audience is mainly young people.*
The German audience have a choice of two music channels.

Here are some other useful collective nouns. Practise using them with singular and plural verbs.

| media | company | public | staff | committee | family |

Speaking: interpreting a chart

5 This chart shows viewing figures for Channel 8 TV. Imagine that you are a Programming Research Analyst at Channel 8. How would you feel about the figures? What action would you take?

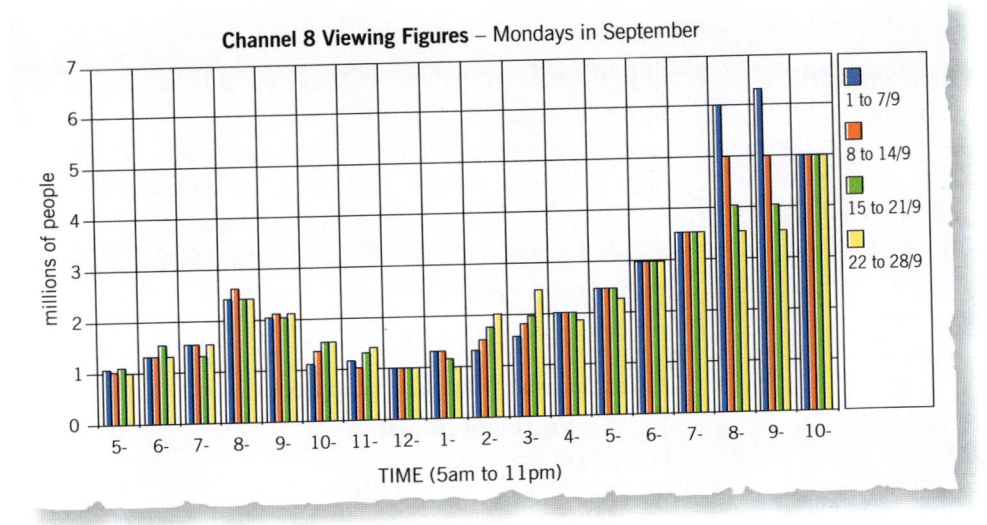

Channel 8 Viewing Figures – Mondays in September

(Chart: millions of people vs TIME (5am to 11pm); legend: 1 to 7/9, 8 to 14/9, 15 to 21/9, 22 to 28/9)

Grammar: so / neither / nor

6 Look at these pairs of sentences about the chart.
- The figures for the 12–1 slot remained the same. So did the figures for the 6–7 slot.
- Viewing figures for the 12–1 slot have not changed. Neither / Nor have the figures for the 6–7 slot.

a What is the function of the second sentence in each pair?
b When do we use *so* and when do we use *neither / nor*?
c In what order are the subject and verb in the second sentences? Rewrite the second sentences, beginning, *The figures ...*

7 Add a sentence beginning with *so*, *neither* or *nor* about the chart.
a The 5–6 slot is not popular.
b The audience for the 8–9 slot fell steadily.
c The programmes in the 8–9 slot have not been successful.
d The new 10 a.m. programme looks good.

▶▶ p.85 **Grammar backup 10**

Speaking: describing a chart

8 Read the beginning of a short talk describing the chart. Then continue it.

'These are the viewing figures for Mondays in September. The coloured bars show audience figures for different weeks – the blue is the first week, red is the second and so on. The figures reveal some good news and some bad news. First the good news. The 10 a.m. slot shows a steady rise in the number of viewers, and so do a number of other slots ...'

Writing: summarising information from a chart.

9 Imagine you have to write a very short report to the head of production, highlighting important information in the chart. Complete 2 and 3 below.

MEMO

To: Head of Production
From: Claudia

I enclose viewing figures for Mondays in September.

1. The 10–11 a.m. slot: *The audience has risen steadily from 1.2 million in the week beginning September 1st to 1.5 million in the w/b September 22nd.*
2. The 2–4 p.m. slot: .....
3. The 8–10 p.m. slot: .....

Word file Unit 10

MARKETING
agency *n*
campaign *n*
competitor *n*
corporate *adj*
event *n*
feedback *n*
findings *n pl*
press release *n*
project *n*
promotion *n*
research *n*

TELEVISION
dip *n/v*
peak *n/v*
ratings *n pl*
scheduling *n*
time slot *n*

VERBS
analyse *v*
assemble *v*
carry out *v*
combine *v*
conduct *v*
draw up *v*

find out *v*
go ahead *v*
plot *v*
put forward *v*
put together *v*
set up *v*
take on *v*
talk over *v*
target *n/v*
try out *v*
tune in / out *v*
turn on / off *v*

SOCIAL ISSUES
drugs *n pl*
immigration *n*
law and order *n*
marriage *n*
politics *n pl*
racism *n*
religion *n*
sexism *n*

OTHER WORDS
initiative *n*
issue *n*
outcome *n*

Grammar backup 10

Phrasal verbs

Practice

1 Read the text. Replace the verbs in brackets with the correct form of the phrasal verbs below.

| fill in   ~~carry out~~   set up   draw up |
| go ahead   find out   take on   put together |
| put forward |

Our company has decided (a) *to carry out* (to do) some research into what our customers think of our products. We want (b) ..... (to discover) what they like and dislike and then we (c) ..... (will assemble) a report with our findings. We have decided that the best way to do this is (d) ..... (to prepare) a questionnaire which we will ask our customers (e) ..... (to complete). Then we (f) ..... (will organise) interviews with some of the customers to get more detailed information. To do this, we (g) ..... (will employ) extra staff for two weeks. Once we have analysed all the information, senior management (h) ..... (will suggest) a plan at a special meeting and hopefully we (i) ..... (will start) with any new developments at the beginning of next year.

2 Correct the mistakes.

a We're going to find about new markets out.
   We're going to find out about new markets.
b This meeting is important. We must set up it as soon as possible.
c Why don't we go ahead interviews next week?
d I'm sorry I haven't finished the report yet. I'll put together it this afternoon.

3 Translation

Write these sentences in your own language. Then close your Course Book. Translate the sentences back into English.

a We should go ahead with our plan.
b Let's set up the interviews for next month.
c They haven't taken on new staff yet.
d We could draw up a questionnaire.
e Most companies carry out salary reviews every year.
f He put forward a new proposal last week.
g I can put together a report for you by lunch time.

Reference

- Phrasal verbs (verbs with an adverb or preposition) often have specific meanings that are difficult to guess from their individual parts. They are very common in informal spoken English: *He **called off** (cancelled) the meeting. They need to **take on** (employ) more staff. They're going to **draw up** (prepare) a questionnaire.*

- Here are three types of phrasal verbs.

  Phrasal verbs that take no object:
  The meeting **went ahead**.
  I often **get up** late.

  Separable phrasal verbs that take an object:
  They've **set up the meeting** for tomorrow.
  They've **set the meeting up** for tomorrow.
  They've **set it up** for tomorrow.

  An object noun can come before or after the adverb: *We're going to **take more staff on**. We're going to **take on more staff**.* An object pronoun must come between the verb and adverb: *We're going to **take them on**.*

  Inseparable phrasal verbs that take an object:
  Look after these papers.
  Look after them.

  The object (noun or pronoun) must come after the preposition: *He's **looking after the children** / **them** today.*

84

So / neither / nor

Practice

1 Reply to the statements a – h with the sentences below.

> ~~Neither do I!~~   Neither are the managers!
> I think we should!   So am I.   We can!
> So should we.   So did Cable Worldwide.
> Neither have we.

a   He doesn't like working full-time.
    Neither do I!
b   They've never used an agency before.
c   We issued a press release last week.
d   They can't analyse the figures until next week.
e   She's going to talk over the problem with the marketing department.
f   The sales representatives aren't working very efficiently at the moment.
g   We shouldn't employ any more staff at the moment.
h   They should spend more money on development.

2 Add information using *so / neither / nor*.

a   We've just had a pay rise.   *So have we.*
b   I hear that Georgio has got
    a new car.   ..... Marina.
c   I can't come to the reception.   ..... Mr Woods.
d   He won't return my calls.   ..... his secretary.
e   You shouldn't work so hard.   ..... you.
f   They visited us at the office
    last week.   ..... their colleagues.
g   I'm really pleased to see you.   ..... I.

3 Add information with statements about *yourself*.

a   'I can speak three languages.'
b   'I'd like to visit London.'
c   'I've never lived abroad.'
d   'I don't like learning English.'

Reference

- We use *so* + auxiliary / modal verb + subject to add similar information to a positive statement. *So* means the same as *too*: *The report is ready and **so** are the invitations.* (They are too.) *They have finished their report. **So** have we.* (We have too.)

- We use *neither / nor* + auxiliary / modal verb + subject to add information to a negative statement. *Neither / nor* means *also not*. *Nor* and *neither* have the same meaning: *Silvano hasn't phoned yet.* ***Neither / Nor*** *has Dieter.* (Dieter also hasn't.)

- To add contrasting information to a positive or negative statement, we can use a subject + auxiliary verb.

Statement	Additional Information	Contrasting Information
Their sales went up last year.	So did Timson's.	Ours didn't!
I'm not happy about this.	Neither is my boss.	We are!
We can't wait much longer.	Nor can our customers.	We can!

- The additional or contrasting information can be included in the same sentence: *Their sales went up last year but **ours didn't**.*

4 Translation

Write these sentences in your own language. Then close your Course Book. Translate the sentences back into English.

a   I must speak English at work. So must my boss.
b   She's never visited New York. Neither has her family.
c   He uses his e-mail all the time but I don't.
d   They aren't going to the conference but I am.

Media

At work

11

- Read and talk about conditions of employment
- Listen to an interview
- Interview someone and report your findings
- Vocabulary: working lives
- Grammar: passive structures with *get*

Action A — Working conditions

Reading and Speaking: conditions of employment

1 Read about two people's experiences of working in Britain. Discuss differences between their conditions of employment and conditions in your country.

'I do temporary work through an agency – you know, secretarial or clerical work. I go to a lot of different companies and organisations, usually covering for people on holiday. The employer doesn't pay me direct – they pay the agency and the agency pays me. It's difficult to take days off because I don't get paid for them, but if I work weekends or public holidays I get double the usual hourly rate.'

'I have an administrative job in the contracts department of a monthly magazine and I do a five-day week, Monday to Friday. I sometimes have to work late on weekdays, but the office is closed on Saturdays and Sundays. I start at about nine in the morning, have an hour for lunch at about 12.30, then finish at 5.30. We usually have short mid-morning and mid-afternoon breaks. Holidays are three weeks a year, and I can take them when I want them. Then there are public holidays at Christmas, New Year and Easter – and a few in the summer too. The salary's not bad and I sometimes get a bonus at the end of the year.'

Vocabulary: working lives

2 Look at the words below.

a Group them under these headings. Use a dictionary to help you. Can you add any other words under each heading?
- Employers • Jobs • Type of contract • Money • Free time

pay	part-time	secretarial	wage	full-time	holidays
bonus	organisation	temporary	permanent	day off
salary	public holidays	break	company	clerical	agency
administrative	hourly rate

b Choose words from the list to complete this job description.
'I work for a large [1] ..... in the centre of the city. It's an [2] ..... job, so I spend most of my day dealing with routine paperwork. It's only [3] ..... at the moment, while my son is small – I leave at two. I still have [4] ....., though – three weeks, plus [5] ..... . I get paid monthly and the [6] ..... is quite good.'

c Think of a job that you know well. Use the words from your lists to describe that job.

86

Unit **11A**

Listening to an interview

3 Eva Hiltner is German. She works at MTV Europe providing customer service to commercial clients. She describes some differences between working in Germany and Britain. Discuss what these differences might be. Then listen and compare your answers.

a Which country offers more opportunities to young people, in Eva's opinion?

b In which country:
  • is it usual to stay in the same job for a very long time?
  • do young people have more power?
  • do young people earn more money?
  • do people work longer hours?
  • do people not usually work at weekends?

c Eva uses two expressions a lot: *you know* and *I mean*. Why does she use these expressions? What does she use them for?

Grammar: passive structures with *get*

4 Look at these extracts from the interviews in Exercises 1 and 3.

*I **get paid** only for the days I actually work.*
*You just wait until eventually you **get promoted**.*

a If you *get paid* do you pay someone or does someone pay you?

b If you *get promoted* do you get a better job or do you give someone a better job?

c Which words can replace *get* in these extracts?

d Which verb form follows *get* in this passive structure?

5 Rephrase these sentences using the same tense of a passive structure with *get*. The person doing the action is not important.

a 'Nobody cleans the offices regularly.'
   The offices don't get ...
b 'The company sacked her last week.'
c 'The men damaged some of the computers in the move.'
d 'Someone's locked our coats in the studio.'
e 'They moved him to a different department last week.'
f 'The boss gives me all the difficult jobs.'

▶▶ p.92 **Grammar backup 11**

Talking point

> PEOPLE SHOULD RETIRE AT 45 AND GIVE THEIR JOBS TO YOUNGER PEOPLE.

What do *you* think?

Speaking and Writing: interviewing and reporting

6 Interview someone in the class (including your teacher) about their working life. Find out about:
  • Pay • Hours • Overtime • Holidays
  • Promotion • Job changes

Write a report on your findings.

7 Outside the classroom, interview an elderly person who can tell you about working conditions in the past or someone who has worked abroad and can tell you about conditions there. Report your findings to the class.

Media

Action B **Working abroad**

- Read an article
- Interview someone
- Read and write a CV and a letter of application
- Grammar: present perfect continuous

Reading a magazine article

1 Look at the picture below and say what you think.

a What is this man's profession?
b Where is he from?
c Where does he live?
d Where does he work?

2 Now read the article and check your answers.

3 What information does the article give about Simón's:
- education?
- past jobs?
- present activities?
- skills?

Simón el Rubio

DANCER

'I'm half Czech and half English. Both my parents were ballet dancers so I grew up in the theatre. They knew how difficult a dancer's life could be and they certainly didn't want me to become one.

'They encouraged me to go to university, where I studied law and languages. But I was also interested in music and continued with that – the violin and piano at first, and later the guitar. It was through the guitar that I became aware of flamenco. When I heard that the famous Spanish guitarist Paco de Lucia was coming to London, I had to see him. I was amazed at what I heard. I knew then that I had to get to Andalucia and find out more about flamenco.

'After leaving university, I became a solicitor for a short time, but I soon gave it up to follow my artistic ambitions. I travelled to Córdoba and studied flamenco guitar and dance and later made my home in Estepona on the south coast of Spain. I learned the hard way, playing in small clubs and restaurants, all the time developing my skills and technique. By the time I had spent all my savings I was much closer to living the flamenco way of life. A gypsy once said to me, "Simón, you'll never understand flamenco until you understand what it's like to be poor." Now I know. It has sharpened all my senses.

'I'm very lucky because I've been accepted by the flamenco community in Estepona. I've been going to flamenco festivals for many years and I've seen the best performers in Spain. Often I'm the only foreign performer there.

'Now I have my own dance company and we've been on three tours in Asia. The current show is a theatrical presentation of flamenco and tango. We've been touring with *Heartbeat* since 1995 and we've given hundreds of performances. My ambition is to take the company to the best theatres in the world.'

Grammar: present perfect continuous

4 Look at these two extracts from the article. Answer the questions below.

I've been going to flamenco festivals for many years ...
We've been touring with Heartbeat since 1995.

a When did Simón start going to Flamenco festivals? Does he still go to them now?
b When did his company start touring with Heartbeat? Are they still doing the show?
c Why is *for* used with one time phrase and *since* used with the other?
d How is the present perfect continuous formed?
e Write questions that the two sentences above can answer. *How long ...?*
f Find two examples in the text of the present perfect simple. Why does the writer use this form rather than the present perfect continuous?

▶▶ p.93 **Grammar backup 11**

CURRICULUM VITAE

Surname:	Hansen
First name:	Anne
Address:	27A Belmont Gardens London SW12 2AS
Telephone:	0181 330 0798
Date of birth:	June 20th 1973 Female
Nationality:	Danish

Educational qualifications:

1996   BA (English and Business Studies) University of London

Career history:

1996 — now   Researcher at UKTV, London (Senior researcher since 1998)

Interests:
- Foreign languages: English, French, Spanish
- Music (member of orchestra since 1995)
- Marathon running
- Working with young people (acting as a counsellor on an inner-city youth project for the last two years)

5 Read the CV and letter below. Write questions and answers about Anne Hansen using the present perfect continuous.

EXAMPLE: live in England? *How long has she been living in England? For five years.*

a play in an orchestra?
b work for UKTV?
c work as a senior researcher?
d counsel young people?

Speaking: interviews

6 Work in pairs. Use a variety of tenses.

A: Interview your partner. Ask questions to complete a CV like the one on the left.
B: Answer with true information about yourself. Then change roles.

Writing a letter of application

7 Look again at the letter below. Discuss these questions.

a What is the purpose of each paragraph?
b Why does the writer end with *Yours faithfully*? When do we use *Yours sincerely*?

8 Write a letter of application for a job that interests you. Say where you saw it advertised and enclose your CV.

27A Belmont Gardens
London SW12 2AS

April 26th

Dear Sir/Madam,

I am writing to apply for the post of **Programme Researcher** as advertised in the London News on April 24th.

I come from Denmark but I have been living in London for the last five years. I did a degree in English and Business Studies at London University and since then I have been working as a researcher for a television company.

I enclose my CV and look forward to hearing from you.

Yours faithfully,

Anne Hansen

Anne Hansen

Media

Action C — Interviews

- Read a job advertisement
- Talk about interviews
- Listen to an extract from a talk on interview techniques
- Listen to an extract from a job interview
- Interview someone
- Present yourself
- Vocabulary: personal qualities

Reading a job advertisement

1 Look at the advertisement below.

a What organisation is offering the jobs?
b Are the jobs permanent or temporary, part-time or full-time?
c What different jobs are available? What do you think they involve?
d What kind of people are they looking for?
e If you are interested, what do you do next?

2 Imagine you are going to interview candidates for the jobs below.

a What professional skills are you looking for?
b What experience should candidates have?

KEYCAMP Holidays

Work in holiday locations throughout Europe

Keycamp Holidays is one of the UK's largest self-drive camping and mobile home tour operators. We are looking for independent, sociable and enthusiastic people who would welcome the opportunity to work in an outdoor environment for 3-6 months this summer.

The following positions are available:

CAMPSITE COURIER: Minimum age 18 years, full or half season. The opportunity to work in an enjoyable holiday atmosphere while providing a first class service to our clients. Knowledge of French, Spanish, Italian or Dutch is an advantage.

CHILDREN'S COURIER: Minimum age 18 years, required May to September. Are you creative and do you enjoy working with children? This position gives you the chance to use your talents to organise activities for children aged 4–13 years. Previous experience working with children is essential.

SITE SUPERVISOR/SENIOR COURIER: Minimum age 21 years, full season. Responsible for co-ordinating courier activity and for the presentation of the Keycamp product on site. Previous experience in managing groups of young people is desirable. The ability to speak French, Spanish, Italian or Dutch is essential.

Accommodation, uniform and training provided. Rates of pay are competitive.

To request a detailed job description and application form, telephone or write to:

Susan Parchment,
Overseas Personnel Manager, Keycamp Holidays,
92-96 Lind Road, Sutton, Surrey, SM1 4PL
Telephone: 0181-395 8170

---

3 What personal qualities do candidates need? Choose five qualities for each job from this list, and from other adjectives that you know. Use a dictionary to help you.

enthusiastic	independent	cooperative	generous	forceful
motivated	creative	kind	lively	honest	patient
sociable	hard-working	energetic	well-organised	quiet
open-minded	efficient	well-travelled	calm	

Speaking: interviews

4 Remember a job interview that you have had (or imagine an interview for a job you would like).

a What kinds of questions were you asked?
b Did you ask any questions? What were they about?
c How did you present yourself? Why?

Listening: interview techniques

5 🔊 **Alison Turvey trains people to improve their interview skills.**

a What interview techniques and strategies will she say are important, do you think? Think about these areas:
- appearance
- knowledge of the company
- body language
- how you speak
- what you say

b Listen to Alison's advice, and make notes under these headings.
- Preparing for the interview
- At the interview
  – appearance   – speaking   – questions

EXAMPLE: *Find out about the company.*

c Do you agree with this advice?

d Give examples of what you consider to be positive and negative body language.

Listening to an extract from a job interview

6 🔊 **Job applicants are often asked, 'Why do you think you are suitable for this job?' Listen to someone answering this about a Keycamp Holidays job.**

a Listen once. Which job is he applying for?

b Listen again. In which order does he mention:
- his personal qualities?
- his skills?
- his experience?

How does he introduce each of these topics?

c What do we know about the candidate's:
- education?
- foreign language skills?
- leadership skills?

d Do you think this person is a strong candidate for the job? Why/why not?

Phrasebook

Presenting yourself

I've been working with computers.
I've got quite a lot of experience of working in Europe.
I've had experience of the leisure industry.
I've got a background in hotel work.
I'm interested in other cultures.
I'm interested in working with young people.
I'm capable of working alone.
I'm familiar with the company's image.
I've been studying business management.

Speaking: interviewing

7 Work in pairs.

a Prepare to interview your partner for a job with Keycamp Holidays, and then to be interviewed.
Interviewer: Ask the applicant why they think they are suitable. Ask for more information if you need to.
Applicant: Explain why you are suitable for the job. Use expressions from the *Phrasebook* to help you.

b Change partners and repeat the interview process. Then discuss in your groups of four why particular applicants were or were not suitable.

Word file   Unit 11

JOBS
ad**mi**nistrative *adj*
clerical *adj*
co**or**dinate *v*
counsel *v*
counsellor *n*
courier *n*
leisure industry *n*
manage *v*
re**sear**cher *n*
secre**tar**ial *adj*
site su**per**visor *n*
so**li**citor *n*
tour operator *n*

WORKING CONDITIONS
bonus *n*
break *n*
day **off** *n*
overtime *n*

public **hol**iday *n*
re**tire** *v*
savings *n pl*
wages *n pl*

PERFORMANCE
ballet dancer *n*
festival *n*
gui**ta**rist *n*
orchestra *n*
tech**nique** *n*
the**a**trical *adj*
tour *n*

QUALITIES
am**bi**tion *n*
capable *adj*
cre**a**tive *adj*
diplo**ma**tic *adj*
enthusi**as**tic *adj*
i**ni**tiative *n*

sensitive *adj*
sociable *adj*
talent *n*

COMPUTING
database *n*
software
    package *n*
spreadsheet *n*
word-processing *n*

OTHER WORDS
background *n*
body language *n*
desirable *adj*
e**ssen**tial *adj*
fa**mi**liar *adj*
graduate *n*
im**pressed** *adj*
strategy *n*

Grammar *backup 11*

Passive structures with *get*

Practice

1 Fill in the gaps with an appropriate expression using *get* and the past participle of one of the verbs below.

| dress | catch | invite | ~~break~~ | lose | stop |
| change | marry | damage | pay | promote |
| steal |

a The glass *got broken* when I dropped it yesterday.
b We'd like to ..... in a church.
c I need to ..... before I go to the reception. These clothes aren't smart enough.
d I often ..... to business receptions but I don't often go.
e Hurry up and ..... or you'll be late for school again.
f I ..... by the customs officer when I arrived at Heathrow Airport last week but he didn't find anything.
g I ..... when I went to their new offices last week because I hadn't been there before.
h I hope I ..... soon because I haven't got any money.
i I was lucky that my jewellery ..... when my flat was burgled last week.
j I'm sure that she's ..... next week to Head of Department – she's the best person for the job.
k The roof ..... in the storm last week.
l The thief ..... by the police after a car chase.

2 Translation

Write these sentences in your own language. Then close your Course Book. Translate the sentences back into English.

a I get paid once a month.
b They're getting married next week.
c We got lost in France.
d She's going to get promoted soon.

Reference

- We use the passive structure *get* + past participle to talk about things that happen often unexpectedly or by accident. We can usually replace *get* with *be*; *get* is more informal: *The things **got / were** damaged in a fire.*

- We also use *get* in some expressions to mean *become*: *We always **get** (become) lost when we drive to London. We're getting married next month.*

- We use *get / have something done* to talk about things which are done for us by someone else. This also has a passive meaning: *I'm **getting** (having) **the figures checked** today.*

Present perfect continuous

Practice

1 Rewrite the sentences without changing the basic meaning, using present perfect simple or continuous verb forms.

a I started queuing at this exchange bureau thirty minutes ago.
   I've been queuing at this exchange bureau for thirty minutes.

b It's been a long time since we last had a meeting.
   We haven't ..... .

c This is his third driving lesson.
   He ..... .

d I usually fly with British Airways; I first travelled with them ten years ago.
   I've ..... .

e I met him six years ago.
   I've ..... .

2 Correct the sentences.

a I've ~~been liking~~ liked her since I was a child.
b She's been going to international conferences since two years.
c It's time to leave work. We were working late every night this week.
d I am living in London since 1978 and I'll never move.
e He's been worked here for two years.
f They haven't been reaching a decision yet.

3 Translation

Write these sentences in your own language. Then close your Course Book. Translate the sentences back into English.

a They've been discussing the problem for hours.
b Who's been using my car? The tank's half empty!
c I haven't been working very hard this week.

Reference

- We use the present perfect continuous, like the present perfect simple, to talk about activities that began in the past and continue up to the present. Using the continuous form emphasises the length of the period: I've been working here for six months. If a situation has become permanent or is lasting a very long time, we usually use the present perfect simple instead: I've lived in Madrid all my life.

- Even if a situation has continued for a very long time, we use the present perfect continuous to talk about regular activities that are still continuing: He's **been going** to festivals for years.

- The present perfect simple is used to talk about completed actions at an unspecified time in the past: I've been to Bali. However, the present perfect continuous can be used to talk about recent completed actions: I've been visiting friends all day. **Have** you **been crying**?

- Some verbs are rarely or never used in a continuous form (e.g. know, understand, like, love): I've known them for more than a year.

Media

In the news

12

- Talk about presenting news
- Listen to an interview
- Read about a person's career path
- Talk about work experience
- Grammar:
  past perfect

Action A

Presenting

Speaking: presenting news

1 **Think of a news programme you have seen on television.**

a How is it presented? Consider:
   - the age and presentation style of the presenter
   - the content of the programmes
   - the length of news items
   - the use of visual images and background sounds
   - the age of the target audience

b Do you think the news on MTV is presented in the same way?

Listening to an interview

2 **Thomas Madvig is originally from Denmark, but lives and works in London now. He is a news presenter at MTV Europe.**

a Which of these do you think he does as part of his job?
   - edits
   - researches
   - writes
   - makes films
   - interviews
   - finds graphics

b Listen to an interview with him and check your answers.

3 **Listen again. Answer these questions.**

a What are the differences between MTV news and other news programmes?

b Which sources of news does MTV use?
   - TV
   - radio
   - newspapers
   - magazines
   - wires (from news agencies)
   - faxes from correspondents

c How many stories does Thomas usually have to research in one day?

d What time do the news stories have to be ready?

94

Reading: a career path

4 Read these sentences about Thomas's career and put them in the order you think they happened. Then read the text and check your answers.

a His friend suggested trying MTV.
b He worked for radio stations in Denmark.
c Thomas worked on a radio programme at school.
d He came to London to work as a DJ.
e He left school.
f He started presenting news programmes on MTV Europe.

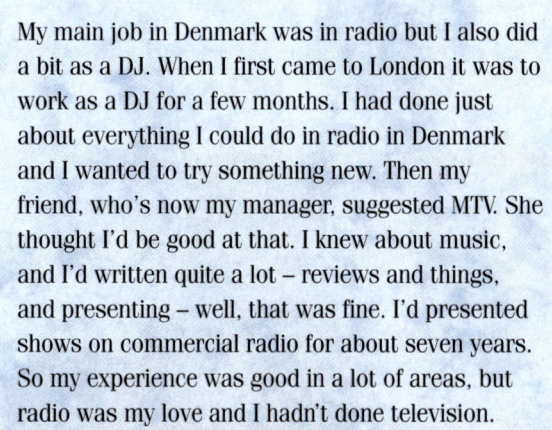

> 'My main job in Denmark was in radio but I also did a bit as a DJ. When I first came to London it was to work as a DJ for a few months. I had done just about everything I could do in radio in Denmark and I wanted to try something new. Then my friend, who's now my manager, suggested MTV. She thought I'd be good at that. I knew about music, and I'd written quite a lot – reviews and things, and presenting – well, that was fine. I'd presented shows on commercial radio for about seven years. So my experience was good in a lot of areas, but radio was my love and I hadn't done television.
> I got interested in radio at school. We had a radio programme that went out at lunch time and I worked on that. Then I dropped out of school to do radio ... because that was what I wanted to do. I worked on commercial radio stations in Denmark ... did some voice-over work and generally got into anything involving radio and media.'

Grammar: past perfect

5 Look at two examples of past perfect verb forms from the text. Answer the questions.

- When I first came to London ... I *had done* just about everything I could do ...
- I knew about music, and I*'d written* quite a lot ...

a When do we use the past perfect? Choose the best ending to this sentence.
- We use the past perfect to refer to ...
  ... an activity that happened in the past.
  ... a recent activity.
  ... an activity that happened before a particular time in the past.

b How is the past perfect formed?

▶ p.100 **Grammar backup 12**

Talking point

NEWS REPORTING CAN NEVER BE OBJECTIVE.

What do *you* think?

6 Work in pairs. Use the prompts below to ask and answer questions about Thomas's experience before he arrived in London.

EXAMPLE: *Had he worked in radio?*
Yes, he had.

a television (work)
b radio programmes (present)
c voice-overs (do)
d reviews (write)
e TV programmes (present)
f news in Danish (read)
g news items in English (write)
h DJ in different countries (be)

Speaking: work experience

7 Work in pairs. Find out what your partner had done before particular points in their life.

EXAMPLE: **A:** *What work had you done before you started your present job?*
B: *I'd only worked in the holidays. I'd been a waiter ...*

Tell the class about your partner.

Media

Action B   Getting it right

- Talk about foreign language use
- Read an interview extract
- Read information from a news agency
- Write and present a news report
- Grammar:
    extended noun phrases

Speaking: foreign language use

1 **In this section, Thomas Madvig talks about his strengths and weaknesses in English. First, discuss the following opinions about foreign language use. Do you agree with them? Why (not)?**

a 'I want my pronunciation to be just like a native speaker's. I don't want people to know that I'm a foreigner.'

b 'It's spoken language that's important. I'm not so worried about my writing.'

c 'It's important to be accurate. If you don't use grammar correctly, you might say something you don't mean.'

d 'When you write something for your job, you have to write it several times. It is important to work at improving it.'

Reading an interview extract

2 **Do you think writing is important in Thomas Madvig's job? What kind of writing do you think he has to do?**

3 **Read the text and answer the questions.**

a Check your answers to Exercise 2.
b What are Thomas's strengths in English?
c What is his biggest weakness?

> Writing is a big thing. I know my grammar's not perfect but I have a good voice and people say my pronunciation's fine. And of course, that's the most important for a presenter. But I have to write too – quite a lot. I write every day – scripts for news items. They go to an editor after I've written them. She corrects them, especially the grammar. My spelling's OK. I don't find that too hard in English. Then the finished scripts are typed on to the autocue for me to read when we're recording the show.

> HOUSTON, April 21 Houston-based company, Celestis, shot ashes of 24 people into space in first space funeral. Included were Gene Roddenberry (Star Trek creator) and Timothy Leary (sixties guru). Pegasus rocket launched at 10,000 kilometres an hour from Lockheed-1011 over Canary Islands. Celestis has thousands of requests from potential clients. Cost $4800. Second launch planned for September.

Reading information from a news agency

4 News readers often write stories based on brief information from news agencies. Look at the text above about the Houston-based company, Celestis.

a What are the main points that make this news item interesting?
b How was the rocket launched?
c Where do you think the plane had originally taken off from?
d If someone wants to send a relative's ashes into space, when can they next do it and how much will it cost?

5 Here is the text after it was made into a story for a radio news programme. Compare the final story with the news agency text above.

a Who is mentioned first in the story? Why is this different from the text above?
b What other changes have been made?

```
The ashes of Star Trek creator Gene
Roddenberry and sixties guru Timothy Leary
rocketed into the final frontier on 21
April in the world's first space funeral.
Their ashes, and those of
22 other people, were aboard a Pegasus
rocket that was blasted into space at
10,000 kilometres an hour from a Lockheed
L-1011 over the Canary Islands. Houston-
based company Celestis, which organised
the space funeral, says it has had
thousands of requests from potential
clients.
It costs $4,800 to send the cremated
remains of a person into space and a
second launch is planned for September.
```

Grammar: extended noun phrases

6 Look at the phrases in italics in the text in Exercise 5.

a Where is the main noun in each phrase? What other kinds of words are used before the main noun to provide extra information?
b Why do you think phrases like these are common in news reports?

7 Change these sentences into news announcements with extended noun phrases. Where is the main noun in each phrase? What nouns and adjectives can go before it?

a *Brad Pitt, who is a Hollywood film star,* is visiting London.
b A man was shot yesterday in Green Street, Bristol. Police are searching for *his girlfriend, who is 40 years old and French.*
c *MTV Europe, which is based in London,* is organising a major youth survey.
d *A Boeing 737 operated by Eurasia Airways* made an emergency landing at Heathrow Airport yesterday.
e *Investment services offered by the People's Bank* are under investigation.

8 Work with your partner and make extended noun phrases by adding nouns and adjectives to the words below. Then finish each sentence to create an imaginary news item.

| manager | computer | footballer | restaurant |
| film | group | Minister | |

EXAMPLE: manager – **store** manager – **department** store manager – **youngest** department store manager – **Britain's** youngest department store manager ...

Britain's youngest department store manager started her new job today on her eighteenth birthday.

▶ p.101 **Grammar backup 12**

Writing and Speaking: presenting a news report

9 Work in groups. Write a news script for a local radio station. Choose three events that you have heard about in the news and write about them in English. Practise reading your script aloud. Then present your news programme to the class.

Media

Action C **Editing skills**

- Talk about reasons for writing
- Recognise types of mistake
- Improve a letter and fax
- Write a fax from notes

Speaking: reasons for writing

1 Imagine you work in a company in your country. Your boss speaks some English but is not confident about writing. Make a list of writing tasks that he / she might ask you to do that involve improving a written text.

EXAMPLE: *Improve the style of a letter written in English.*

Reading: types of mistake

2 Work in pairs. Look at texts A – F (sentences from business letters and an addressed envelope).

a Find mistakes in the texts.
b Match the mistakes with these categories:
- Punctuation
- Grammar
- Vocabulary
- Spelling
- Organisation
- Style

A The package have been sent to you today by courier.

B I enclose an invoise for your order (ref. 23/568).

C Thank you for your letter. Its good to hear from you again.

D IPF International
Ms F White
Westmoor St. 14
SE4 4JT London

E Hello Mr Jones,
   I am writing to apply for the post of Secretary as advertised in the International Herald Tribune on Tuesday, November 4th.

F We will bring the package to you by post.

3 Read the checklist below for improving written texts.

a Why do you think it suggests checking layout, content and organisation first?
b What types of improvements are suggested in STEP 2?
c Why do you think the checklist suggests you check *spelling, punctuation* and *grammar* last?
d Do you think the checklist is useful? Is there anything you would like to change or add?
e What mistakes do *you* often make? Start a separate, personal checklist to use when you check your work.

Checklist for improving written texts

STEP 1 — **Check that the information makes sense**
Read the text once
Is the layout appropriate?
Have you included all the information your reader needs?
Is the information presented in a clear and logical sequence?

STEP 2 — **Check that words and phrases are appropriate**
Read the text again
Have you used any words that are too formal / informal?
Can you replace 'general' words with more specific ones?

Check spelling, punctuation and grammar
Have you made any spelling errors?
Have you used punctuation appropriately?
Have you made any grammatical errors?

Unit **12C**

Writing: improving letters and faxes

4 Look at Text 1 below. Imagine George Stakis is your boss and he wants you to check this letter before you send it out. Work in pairs and improve it. Use the checklist opposite to help you.

1

GKT International
Bahnhofstrasse, 12
München

Dezember 12

Hi Mr Barnett!

I have spoke to our UK representative, patrick donaldson, to contact you about arrange a Meeting as soon as posible. He got Samples of all the things we are making and all our Advertising papers and will be very interest to discussing future possiblties with yourself.

I enclose some Informations about the company.

Thanks to you for your lette of Dezember 8.

Good wishes

George Stakis

George Stakis

5 Look at Text 2. Lay it out as a fax. Work with the checklist and improve the writing, adding any information that is needed on a fax.

2

FAX – Josef Pesti, GKT, Tallinn

I will go in Tallinn on Wednesday january 4th arriving 16.30 from Munich with the Lufthansa plane. Can you to get me a hotel in the centre for Wednesday and Thusday! Please meeting me on the airport.

Thank you

George Stakis

George Stakis

6 Write a fax from the message in Text 3. After writing it, exchange texts with your partner. Work with the checklist and improve your partner's text. Then discuss the changes you have made.

3

I am busy Monday 10th.
Fax Pamela Bradford please.
Change meeting Tuesday 11th. 2-5 p.m.
George

Talking point

THE MESSAGE IN A BUSINESS LETTER HAS TO BE VERY CLEAR.

What do *you* think?

Word file   Unit 12

TELEVISION	review *n*	liberate *v*
audience *n*	script *n*	shoot *v*
autocue *n*	visual *adj*	sum up *v*
correspondent *n*	voice-over *n*	take up *v*
cut *v*	wire *n*	write up *v*
deadline *n*	**VERBS**	**OTHER WORDS**
DJ *n*	assign *v*	ashes *n pl*
edit *v*	blast *v*	frontier *n*
graphics *n pl*	come out with *v*	funeral *n*
image *n*	cremate *v*	potential *adj*
news agency *n*	drop out *v*	rocket *n*
news item *n*	go for *v*	space *n*
present *v*	go on *v*	relative *n*
producer *n*	launch *v*	terrorist *n*
research *n*		

99

Grammar backup 12

Past perfect

Practice

1 Complete the sentences using past perfect simple or past simple verb forms.

a He *felt* (feel) extremely confident before he *went* (go) to the interview.
b As soon as they ..... (test) the computer display, they ..... (try) out the system.
c When the hard disk ..... (crash), he ..... (remember) that he ..... (receive) a guarantee with the computer.
d I ..... (buy) a portable modem when I ..... (be) at the factory outlet last weekend.
e By the time I ..... (arrive) at the stand, all the samples ..... (disappear).
f He ..... (tell) me that he ..... (ask) for promotion before.
g As soon as he ..... (look) at the catalogue entry, he ..... (see) that they ..... (make) a terrible mistake about the price.
h Before you ..... (ask) me, I ..... (be) absolutely convinced that I ..... (answer) all the inquiries about our new product range.

2 Translation

Write these sentences in your own language. Then close your Course Book. Translate the sentences back into English.

a After they'd signed the contract, they went out for a meal to celebrate.
b He realised that he had made a terrible mistake.
c When Maria arrived, David left.
d When Maria arrived, David had left.

Reference

- We use the past perfect to refer to a completed action that happened before another one in the past. It is often used in stories: *It was six o'clock. James **had been** inside all day ...*

- Clauses with past perfect and past simple verbs are often joined by time phrases like *when*, *before*, *after*, *as soon as*, *by the time*: ***By the time** we arrived, they **had eaten** all the food.*

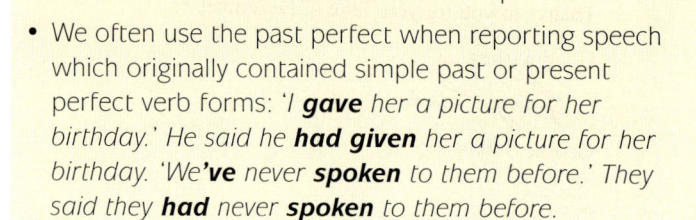

- We often use the past perfect when reporting speech which originally contained simple past or present perfect verb forms: '*I **gave** her a picture for her birthday.*' *He said he **had given** her a picture for her birthday.* '*We**'ve** never **spoken** to them before.*' *They said they **had** never **spoken** to them before.*

When he turned it on, he knew he had done something wrong.

Extended noun phrases

Practice

1 **Shorten the beginnings of sentences 1–7 using extended noun phrases. Then use them to complete sentences a – g below.**

1 Lewis Fashions, which is a successful high street shop ...
2 Angela Lawrence, who is one of Britain's top fashion designers ...
3 The tourist industry in Spain is growing ...
4 Computing Games, which is a mail order company ...
5 Simon Ronson, who is a senior sales manager and multi-lingual ...
6 The latest figures which have been issued by Thompsons from their market research ...
7 Denise Swan, who is a scuba diving champion and internationally famous ...

a Successful high street shop Lewis Fashions has been sold for more than a million pounds.
b ..... announced her retirement yesterday after twenty years in the sport.
c ..... has just launched her own range of children's clothes.
d ..... show that most British households now own at least two television sets.
e ..... is one of the fastest-growing companies in Britain.
f ..... has made history by negotiating a contract in three languages.
g ..... is a result of tour operators reducing their prices by 20%.

2 **Put these extended noun phrases in a logical order. Then write a sentence using the phrase.**

a George, Spanish-speaking, director, Cummins, managing
Spanish-speaking managing director George Cummins didn't need an interpreter when he visited Argentina recently on business.
b Australian, exam, entrance, university
c luggage, lost, department, airport
d Janet Jackson, American, famous, singer

Reference

- In an extended noun phrase we can use nouns and proper names in front of a main noun to give more information:
  policy   insurance **policy**
                office insurance **policy**
  programme recruitment **programme**
                WH Smith recruitment **programme**

- We can use adjectives to describe any of the nouns in the phrase or to describe the whole noun phrase:
  busy car manufacturer (busy manufacturer of cars),
  cheap car manufacturer (manufacturer of cheap cars)

- We also use possessive structures in noun phrases:
  the **company's** marketing plan, the delighted father **of twins**

- We can use noun phrases in front of proper names to identify the person or company: **the Tokyo-based publishing company** English International, **Foreign Affairs Editor** Stephen Ruff

- Extended noun phrases are common in news reports because they are more concise. Compare: *Jeremy Wise, who is a British television producer, is angry and has attacked the government.* (15 words) *Angry British television producer Jeremy Wise has attacked the government.* (10 words)

3 **Translation**

Write these sentences in your own language. Then close your Course Book. Translate the sentences back into English.

a Have you read the new hundred-page marketing report?
b A leading London-based news agency has just launched a new company in South Africa.

Services On line

13

Action A — Intra

- Read an introduction to a company
- Compare marketing methods
- Grammar: linking words

Reading an introduction to a company

1 **Read the text.**

a Explain in not more than 20 words what Intra does. Compare your explanation with a partner's.
b What image of itself do you think the company is communicating through the photograph at the bottom of the page?

WHAT IS INTRA?

INTRA is a Swedish market communications agency, with 27 employees and offices in Uppsala and Stockholm. It works with companies that want to promote themselves or their products and is involved at every stage of a project: establishing a campaign's aims, making suggestions for its content, producing and distributing materials, and evaluating its success.

Intra works with traditional media to sell a client's products or create an image, although it is better known for its use of interactive media. These allow two-way communication between the client and customers. While the choice of media depends on a company's aims, budget and target group, Leif Nordlund, Managing Director of Intra, believes that at least one medium should be interactive.

There are many advantages to Web sites from a company's point of view, so creating them is an important part of Intra's work. Despite being in the far north of Europe, Swedish companies can reach a global audience, particularly if their sites are in English. They know how many people visit their sites, and information can be updated quickly and cheaply.

Of course, companies do need to advertise their Internet address in more traditional ways; the Swedish dairy company Arla, for example, advertised its new site on its milk cartons. The Arla Web site is one that Intra helped to create. The site is extremely popular and includes activities and educational material for children, recipes and the sale of cookery books, as well as campaigns. Arla's breakfast campaign, for instance, reminded people that breakfast is a healthy meal, and a good time for the family to talk to each other.

Intra forms relationships not only with clients but also with suppliers. Some of these suppliers may become partners in a project, with their own project managers – when market research is needed, for example, or highly technical assistance like connecting a Web site to a customer database.

2 Read the text again.

a What are the purposes of:
- a Web site?
- an Internet address?
- a database?

b Which of these are traditional marketing media? Which are interactive? Which can be both? Can you add to the list?
- magazines and newspapers
- television
- the World Wide Web
- direct marketing by mail
- the telephone (telemarketing)
- radio

c How can traditional media include interactive features, do you think?

Grammar: linking words

3 Look at these sentences from the text and the linking words in bold.

- Intra works with traditional media, ... **although** / **though** it is better known for its use of interactive media.
- **While** / **Although** the choice of media clearly depends on a company's aims, ... Leif Nordlund ... believes that at least one medium should be interactive.
- **Despite** / **In spite of** being in the far north of Europe, Swedish companies can reach a global audience.

a What is the function of the words in bold?

b In which sentence can *but* replace the words in bold? What is the usual position of *but* in a sentence?

c What structure follows *despite* / *in spite of*? Rewrite the third example sentence using *although*.

d Look at a different structure which can follow *despite* or *in spite of*. Which words can *although* replace?
- Despite the fact that they are in the far north of Europe, Swedish companies can reach a global audience.

4 Work in pairs. Read these comments by Intra staff. Combine the sentences using the words in brackets, making changes if necessary. Is there more than one possible position for each linking word?

a 'Our offices are both in Sweden. We have international contacts through an association of marketing agencies in Brussels.' (although)

b 'The association is in Brussels. Its correspondence is usually in English.' (but)

c 'Some of our clients are only interested in Swedish customers. They will reach a global audience if they advertise in English.' (while)

d 'I work mainly in Swedish. I need English when I search for information on the Internet.' (despite)

e 'Web site design is interesting. It is difficult to work on a small screen format.' (though)

f 'Many of our Finnish clients are Swedish-speaking. Some prefer to write to us in English.' (in spite of).

▶▶ p.108 **Grammar backup 13**

Speaking: comparing marketing methods

5 Work in groups. Discuss the differences between a television advertisement and a Web site. Which one has more advantages for the customer, do you think? Which is better for the advertiser?

Services

Action B | # The Internet

- Talk about the Internet
- Read Web site pages
- Listen to a talk on Web site design
- Read and write messages
- Vocabulary: computer commands

Speaking: using the Internet

1 Look at this list of things you can do on the Internet.
- Join special interest chat groups
- Play games
- Speak to people over a video phone

a Add other activities to the list.
b Which of the items on your list interest you most? Why?
c Which have you done?
d Do you enjoy using the Internet? Do you find it useful?

Vocabulary: computer commands

2 Look at these verbs. They are all common computer commands. Match each word with an icon below. Use a dictionary to help you.

| connect | open | help | print | save | undo | cut |
| copy | paste | search | view | | | |

3 Now use words from Exercise 2 to complete these sentences.

a You ..... a computer to the Internet by a normal telephone line.
b You can get advice by selecting '.....'.
c If you give a command by mistake you can ..... it.
d The ..... command allows you to see the text as it will be printed.
e To move text from one place to another, you use the ..... command. Then you go to the place where you want the text to be and ..... it there.

Reading Web site pages

4 Look at the introductory page of the Addison Wesley Longman ELT Web site opposite. Discuss these questions in pairs.

a Why do you think the site is presented as a magazine? In what ways is it like one?
b How often do you think the content of this page changes? What makes you think that?
c Which pages (1 – 7) do you think are interactive? What do you think they contain?

104

Unit **13B**

Addison Wesley Longman elt magazine

- About Addison Wesley Longman
- Gateway to Alhambra Longman, Asia Outlook, Dictionaries, Latin America, Longman Hellas, Longman Italia
- For Graphical browsers
- For Text-only browsers

[Quick Search]

1 Longman ELT Readers – Summer Selection
Need a book for the beach? A saga for the seaside? A chronicle for the coast? Read on for suggestions...

2 Decisions, decisions...
Here's some advice on how to choose the best ELT dictionary for you.

3 Ask Alexander
Your questions and the answers from well-known author, Louis Alexander.

4 Ideas for TOEFL Teachers
More advice and another actvitiy to help with TOEFL tests from author, Deborah Phillips.

5 Competitions...
More prizes to be won this month!

6 Latin America
More prizes to be won this month!

7 Other websites
Check out some of our sister companies on the internet.

Listening and Speaking: designing Web sites

5 Look at the chart at the bottom of the introductory Web site page. Which category will you choose to:

a find information on *More Work in Progress*?
b find the name of an author of an AWL book?
c send an e-mail to the company?
d request regular information?
e get news about the company in China?
f take part in a discussion?
g find work?
h locate the nearest company office to you?

6 Sara Lack designs Web sites for her own company. Listen and answer the questions.

a What three main objectives does she mention for a Web site?
b How can a company encourage people to visit a Web site more than once?
c What does Sara think a Web site should contain?
d Now compare the Addison Wesley Longman site with Sara's suggestions.

Note: You can see the up-to-date site at http://www.awl-elt.com

Reading and writing messages

7 You can get access through the Internet to forums on almost any subject. Read message A and the reply to it, message B.

a Imagine message A is about your country. Write an answer like B.
b Choose a country you would like to work in. Write a message like A containing questions you would like answers to.

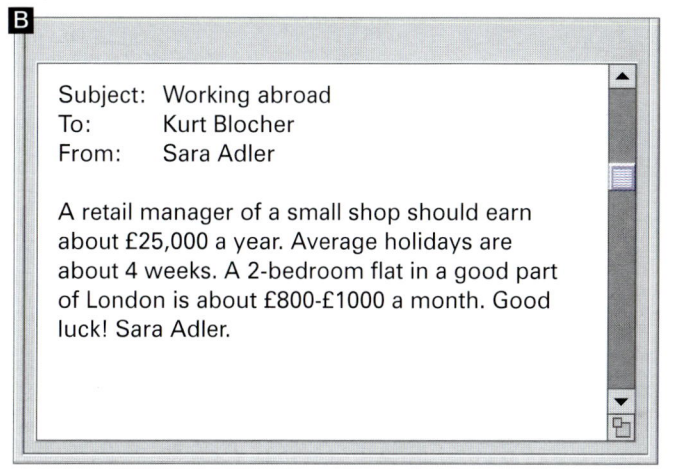

A

Subject: Working abroad
To: All
From: Kurt Blocher

I've been offered a job in London but I don't know if the conditions are good. Can anyone answer these questions? What is an average salary for a manager of a small shop? How many weeks' holiday should I have? How much does it cost to rent a two-bedroom flat? Thanks. Kurt Blocher.

B

Subject: Working abroad
To: Kurt Blocher
From: Sara Adler

A retail manager of a small shop should earn about £25,000 a year. Average holidays are about 4 weeks. A 2-bedroom flat in a good part of London is about £800-£1000 a month. Good luck! Sara Adler.

105

Services

Action C

- Read and talk about fear of technology
- Talk about things you do and do not regret
- Grammar:
   third conditional sentences

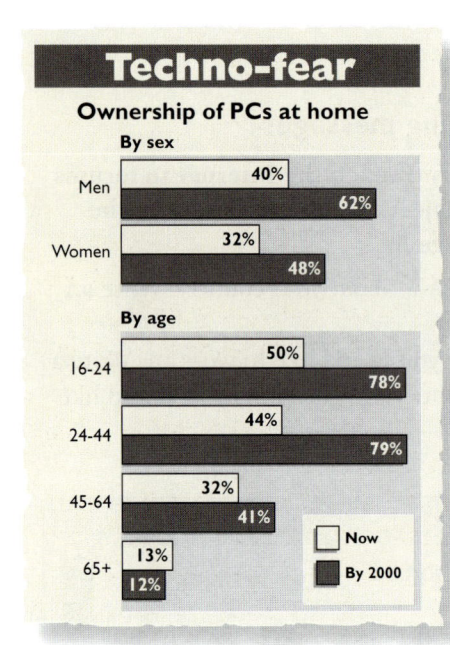

The widening gap

Reading and Speaking: fear of technology

1 Look at the chart below, showing computer use in the UK.

a What does it show about the use of computers by:
   - men and women?
   - younger people and older people?
b What differences does it show between the time when the chart was produced (1996) and the year 2000?
c Give reasons for the differences shown in the chart.
d Do you think that people who do not use computers will be at a disadvantage in the future? If so, in what ways?

2 Read the article below. Answer the questions.

a How do the report's authors think society will be 'divided'?
b In what way is Ron Stanley *switched on* and Susie Vincent *turned off*?
c Why is Susie Vincent worried?
d Are you more like Ron or Susie? Describe your history of working with computers and your attitude to new technology.

Techno-fear

Ownership of PCs at home

By sex
- Men: 40% / 62%
- Women: 32% / 48%

By age
- 16-24: 50% / 78%
- 24-44: 44% / 79%
- 45-64: 32% / 41%
- 65+: 13% / 12%

Now / By 2000

The Great Divide

The information technology revolution is creating a divided society according to a report by the electronics firm, Motorola. Those who have no access to electronic information could be at a disadvantage in the employment market. The report warned that working class and unemployed people, in particular, could fall into the 'information void'. Older people risk missing out on opportunities to make their lives easier, such as on line shopping. 'Having an IT underclass without the means or knowledge to prepare for the future means that society will fall further and further behind in the ability to take advantage of all that information has to offer,' the report says.

Switched on

Ron Stanley's home is full of computer equipment. The 26-year-old accountant admits, 'I feel I have to have the latest thing, the fastest machine that is available.' He was given his first computer when he was 12. 'I loved the games, then when I went to college I started using PCs properly.' He still loves playing games and has recently bought two new games machines. He also has a new PC with Internet connection and fax modem. 'If my parents hadn't given me a computer when I was younger, I probably wouldn't have become so interested in them.'

Turned off

At 35 Susie Vincent feels as if the information revolution has passed her by. 'Computers don't interest me at all. Everybody talks about surfing the net, downloading new software and sending e-mails – it makes me feel so old-fashioned. But I'd prefer to pick up the phone or write a note.' She admits that her dislike of computers is partly caused by fear. 'It annoys me. I am an intelligent, professional woman, but when someone mentions technology my brain switches off. And I feel stupid because I don't understand. My daughter is only ten, but she has no fear of computers. If someone had taught me about them when I was at school, I would have had the confidence to use them. As time passes I feel the gap between people like me and people who understand computers is getting wider and wider. I worry that there are millions of people on the job market who have good computer knowledge. I'm afraid it will damage my chances of moving on or changing jobs.'

Grammar: third conditional sentences

3 Look at these third conditional sentences from the text.

Ron: *If my parents **hadn't given** me a computer when I was younger I probably **wouldn't have become** so interested in them.*

Susie: *If someone **had taught** me about them when I was at school I **would have had** the confidence to use them.*

a Did Ron get a computer when he was young? Did he become interested as a result?
b Was Susie taught about computers at school? Did she become confident about using them?
c When do we use third conditional sentences?
d Look at the verb forms in each clause. How is a third conditional sentence formed?

4 Use information from this text to finish third conditional sentences a – e below.

Lottie didn't do much work at school and she failed some of her exams, so she had to stay at school an extra year. She worked hard and this time she passed them. She went to college to study business administration and learnt English in her spare time. Then she applied for a job with a hotel chain, but she didn't get it because her English wasn't good enough. She decided to go to England for three months to improve her English. She applied for the hotel job again, and this time she got it. Three years later, she's still with the same company. She's going to get married to Lars, who works in the same hotel.

EXAMPLE: *If Lottie had worked harder she would have passed her exams the first time.*

a If she'd passed her exams the first time ..... .
b If she hadn't passed her exams the second time ..... .
c She wouldn't have got the hotel job ..... .
d If her English had been better ..... .
e She wouldn't have met Lars ....

▶▶ p.109 **Grammar backup 13**

Phrasebook

Regrets

I wish I hadn't shouted at him.
If only I'd stayed in my home town.
I'm sorry I didn't work harder.
It's a pity I didn't listen to her.
I regret not tak**ing** that job.
I was wrong to get angry.

No regrets

I'm glad I left when I did.
I don't regret tak**ing** that job.
I was absolutely right to get some extra qualifications.

Speaking: regrets ... no regrets

5 List things you regret doing and things you are glad you did. What was the consequence of each? Explain to the class, using an expression from the *Phrasebook* and a third conditional sentence.

EXAMPLES: (Regret – Lost my temper with a customer. Consequence – Lost my job.)
I wish I hadn't lost my temper. If I'd stayed calm, I wouldn't have lost my job.
(No regrets – Spent a year working for no money at a film company. Consequence – Got a job!)
I'm glad I spent a year working for nothing. If I hadn't done that, I wouldn't have got the job!

Word file Unit 13

MARKETING
communications *n pl*
competition *n*
content *n*
direct marketing *n*
interactive *adj*
market *n*
medium *n*
quiz *n*
special offer *n*
telemarketing *n*
traditional *adj*

THE INTERNET
chatline *n*
download *v*
electronic *adj*

electronics *n*
e-mail *n*
forum *n*
information technology (IT) *n*
on line *adv*
register *v*
surf *v*
Web site *n*
World Wide Web *n*

COMPUTING
click *v*
connect *v*
copy *v*
icon *n*
multimedia *n*

paste *v*
print *v*
save *v*
undo *v*

FEELINGS
fear *n*
glad *adj*
pity *n*
regret *n/v*
wish *v*

OTHER WORDS
budget *n*
despite *prep*
encourage *v*
in spite of *prep*
maintain *v*
up-to-date *adj*

Grammar backup 13

Linking words

Practice

1 Choose the correct linking word in each sentence.

a I didn't buy that mobile phone (but / in spite of) it being on special offer.
b I'd like to learn how to surf the net (despite / despite the fact that) I haven't got a computer!
c (Although / In spite of) I rang him back when I got his message, he'd already left the office.
d I asked my boss for a pay rise (although / despite) knowing that he wouldn't give me one.
e (While / In spite of) I don't mind living in a big city, I'd prefer to move to the country.

2 Fill in the gaps with the linking words below. There is sometimes more than one correct answer.

| in spite of | despite the fact | but | although |
| while | though | | |

a I want to buy a new computer *but* I don't have enough money.
b ..... I ordered our new multimedia system four weeks ago, it still hasn't arrived.
c ..... that his hard disk has crashed three times before, he doesn't back up his files regularly.
d ..... the training programme, many of our staff still do not know how to use e-mail.
e ..... no one visited our Web site three months ago, now we are getting 100 visitors a day!
f I really like you ..... I don't know why!

3 Rewrite the sentences so that they have the same meaning.

a Although it was raining, I went out for a walk.
Despite the rain, I went out for a walk.
b He went on holiday in spite of having no money.
Although ..... .
c Despite the fact that she got up very early, she missed her flight.
In spite of ..... .
d In spite of trying hard, we were not able to complete the job.
While ..... .

Reference

- We use *although*, *though*, *despite*, *in spite of*, *but* and *while* to join two clauses and contrast two statements: *My fax modem broke down **although** it was almost new. **While** our sales continue to rise, we need to improve customer services.*

- We use *although*, *though*, *while*, *despite*, *in spite of* before or after the first clause. We can only use *but* between two clauses: *In spite of having e-mail at work, I prefer to use the phone. I prefer to use the phone at work, in spite of having e-mail. I have e-mail at work but I prefer to use the phone.*

- We use a subject / verb clause after *although*, *though*, *despite the fact that*, and *while*: ***Although** International Electronics is a new company, it is doing very well.* We use a noun, pronoun or *-ing* form after *in spite of* and *despite*: ***In spite of being** a new company, International Electronics is doing very well.*

4 Translation

Write these sentences in your own language. Then close your Course Book. Translate the sentences back into English.

a In spite of the cost, I'm going to Australia on holiday.
b I have to travel in my job although I don't want to.
c While it's a good idea to save money, it's also nice to spend it!

Third conditional sentences

Practice

1 Write a conditional sentence for each situation

a I fell asleep. I didn't hear the phone.
   If I hadn't fallen asleep, I would have heard the phone.

b The spare parts arrived late. We couldn't deliver them.
   If ..... .

c We worked until midnight. We finished the job.
   If ..... .

d He didn't write the report. You didn't ask him.
   He ..... .

e She didn't go to the meeting. Her car broke down on the motorway.
   She ..... .

2 Complete the sentences.

a If only I had ..... .
b I wish my neighbours hadn't ..... .
c I would have ..... .
d If my boss had ..... .

3 Correct the mistakes.

a If you had ~~leave~~ *left* a contact number, I would have been able to phone you.

b If they would have placed their order earlier, they would have received the machines by now.

c She would got the job if her English had been better.

d If we had a stand at last month's exhibition, we might have won their order.

e If I hadn't gone to the conference in Vienna, I wouldn't have meet my future employer.

f I wish I saved more money when I was working.

g What had you done if you had been me?

Reference

- We use the third conditional to talk about events or situations which happened in the past and cannot be changed, or about imaginary events. We are thinking about situations that were possible but did not happen: *If I had filed the document, I wouldn't have lost it.* (But I didn't file it, so I lost it. This cannot be changed.)

- We also use the third conditional to talk about regrets or missed opportunities in the past. We use *I wish / If only* with a similar meaning. *If only* is more emphatic than *I wish*: *If I hadn't eaten so much, I wouldn't have felt ill. **I wish / If only** I hadn't eaten so much. I wouldn't have felt ill.*

- We form the third conditional with *if* + past perfect, + *would* + *have* + past participle. We can use *could* or *might* instead of *would* if we are less certain about the result: *If they had left earlier, they **would** have caught their flight.* (certain) *If they had left earlier, they **could / might** have caught their flight.* (possible)

- There are two parts to a third conditional sentence. The *if* clause can come before or after the main clause: *What would you have done **if you had lost all your work on disk**? **If you had lost all your work on disk**, what would you have done?*

- We use contracted forms in spoken English: *If **you'd** (juːd) asked me earlier, **I'd have** (aɪdəv) told you. If she **hadn't** (hædənt) been so rude, I **wouldn't have** (wʊdəntəv) lost my temper.*

4 Translation

Write these sentences in your own language. Then close your Course Book. Translate the sentences back into English.

a If they had offered me promotion, I might have taken it.

b What would you have done if you'd lost your job?

c We wouldn't have missed the plane if the taxi hadn't broken down.

Services
Our environment

14

Action A

- Discuss environmental problems
- Listen to an interview
- Listen and take notes
- Write from notes
- Make recommendations
- Vocabulary: resources

Policies

Speaking: environmental problems

1 **Look at the pictures above and discuss these questions.**

a What negative effects are these individuals and companies having on their environment?
b What negative effects can people who work in offices have on their environment?
c What positive things can we do at work to reduce these effects?

2 **What do these expressions mean? Use a dictionary to help you.**

- an environmental policy
- goals
- environmental damage

Listening to an interview

3 **Intra takes environmental concerns very seriously. Listen to Björn Falkanäs, Intra's art director.**

a What has Intra already changed about its working practices?
b Why does the company employ a consultant?
c What two reasons does Björn give for the company's attitude?
d How does Intra's attitude affect other companies?

Vocabulary: resources

4 **Match the words below to the four headings. Then add two other words or phrases to each list. Use a dictionary to help you.**

ENERGY   TRANSPORT   MATERIALS   PACKAGING

boxes   paint   lorries   heating   electricity   trains
polystyrene   chemicals

5 Look at the adjectives below.

a Which adjectives are positive? Which are negative? Use a dictionary to help you.

> harmful   poisonous   recyclable   noisy   reusable
> environmentally-friendly   safe   toxic   damaging   wasteful
> renewable   clean   polluted   dirty   green

b Use the adjectives to describe the resources that you listed in Exercise 4.

Listening and Writing: taking notes

6 A British company has invited a consultant to talk to staff about the environment.

a Listen and complete the notes below.

	Definition	Action
A INPUT	= the resources that we use	• Find better resources. • Persuade suppliers to provide them. • Persuade suppliers to use less packaging.
B PROCESS	=	• ..... e.g. Switch off machines, fill delivery lorries.
C	= our products and waste materials	• ..... • Find a company that can use waste as raw material. • .....

b Listen again. What expressions does the speaker use:
  • to list points?   • to introduce a definition of a word?

Talking point

WHY SHOULD I THINK ABOUT THE ENVIRONMENT? I CAN'T MAKE A DIFFERENCE.

What do *you* think?

Writing from notes

7 Use the notes from Exercise 6 to report the consultant's advice for the company newsletter. Start like this:

A visiting consultant advised staff that every company should consider three main areas of its work in relation to the environment. The first area is input ...

Services

Action B

- Read and write minutes
- Listen to meetings
- Make recommendations
- Grammar:
  future perfect

Decisions

Speaking: minutes of a meeting

1 Formal notes about a meeting are called *minutes*.

a Why do we take minutes? What are they for?
b What information do you think minutes should contain?

Listening to a meeting

2 Vision Design Limited has set up a small group to develop an environmental policy for the company. Listen to their first meeting.

a What are the four main points on the agenda?
b What decision is made about each point?

Reading minutes

3 Look at the three sets of minutes, A – C.

a Which minutes do you think are best? Why?

A

VISION DESIGN LTD

Environmental Group Meeting, 8.12.98

Apologies	– MP in another meeting
Consultant	– Mary Hill, Green Alert? (PJ to contact)
Information	– news-sheet for all staff (AB)
	– minutes to directors
Finances	– Group to make formal proposal to directors
Meetings	– 4.30, 2nd Thursday of month

B

VISION DESIGN LTD

The Environmental Group met last Thursday, although Maggie was in another meeting and could not come.

First the Group discussed possible consultants to help the Group set goals for the company. People suggested representatives from Green Alert, Efficient Living and Our Earth.

Then they talked about communication within the company. This is very important, so Anne will prepare a news-sheet each month and give everyone a copy; the directors must have one too.

The next discussion was about money. Clearly an environmental policy is going to cost the company a lot, but that is not a problem.

The next Group meeting will be on Thursday, January 14th at half past four.

C

VISION DESIGN LTD

Minutes of the Environmental Group Meeting held on 8 December 1998

Present: Anne Byron (AB), Peter Jones (PJ), Len Page (LP)
Minutes: Carol Pearson (CP)
Apologies: Maggie Price

1 Appointment of a consultant
Various names were proposed. PJ will ask Mary Hill of Green Alert to attend the next meeting to discuss her possible involvement in setting goals. ACTION PJ.

2 Communication within the company
All staff should be consulted and informed about developments. AB will produce a monthly news-sheet. Carol will copy minutes of Group meetings to company directors. ACTION AB, CP.

3 Financial support
LP reported that the company directors are happy to pay for the design and implementation of an environmental policy. However, they have asked the Group to make a proposal before a consultant is formally hired. This proposal will be made after discussions with the consultant.

4 Future meetings
The Group agreed to meet at 4.30 on the second Thursday of each month. The next meeting will be on January 14.

Unit **14B**

b Which of these statements about minutes do you think are true?
Good minutes ...
- are clear, brief and correct.
- contain a record of everything that was said.
- are organised under headings, following the points on the agenda.
- include a record of people attending.
- contain action points.
- need to be understood only by people who were at the meeting.

Grammar: future perfect

4 Look at this sentence from the meeting.

I'll have calculated the cost by next Wednesday's directors' meeting.

a Does Anne already know what the cost of a news-sheet is?
b Will she know before next Wednesday?
c Do we know exactly when she will find out?
d How is the future perfect formed?

5 Look again at the minutes in C. What will these people have done by the next Environmental Group meeting? Write sentences about:

a Peter
b Anne
c Carol

6 Work in pairs. Discuss what you have done since last week. What will you have achieved by the end of this week? What will you *not* have done? Why?

EXAMPLE: *I'll have had a job interview. I won't have paid my rent, because ...*

▶▶ p.116   **Grammar backup 14**

Listening and Writing: minutes

7 Listen to a meeting of the directors of Vision Designs Limited. The directors are Sam Tenby, John Lane and Penny Wright. Anne Byron was also invited to attend.

a Listen once and write down the main headings for your minutes.
b Listen again and note down the main points under each heading.
c Work with a partner. Compare your notes and write the minutes of the meeting.

Speaking: making recommendations

8 Two recommendations were made in response to Vision Design's practical and environmental problem of car parking:

Some of them (the staff) *should share cars ...*
She (Anne) *could suggest alternatives ...*

Discuss other possibilities, and then make a list of recommendations for the company. Use phrases from the *Phrasebook* to help you.

Phrasebook

Making recommendations

You should switch off lights when you leave a room.
We could use less paper.
Why don't they use different bins for their waste?
We would use fewer resources **if** people sometimes worked at home.
It would be better to control the heating in each room **instead of** centrally.
A better way to deliver documents locally **would be** by bicycle.

113

Services

| Action | C | **In the home** |

- Talk about waste disposal
- Read about a local campaign
- Discuss proposals
- Vocabulary:
  projects
- Grammar:
  -ing forms

Speaking: waste disposal

1 Look at the picture and the extract from a household questionnaire. Work in pairs.

a Match the objects in the picture to categories of waste in the questionnaire.

Which waste products do you separate out for recycling?
- [ ] glass
- [ ] paper
- [ ] vegetable/garden waste
- [ ] plastic
- [ ] metal
- [ ] clothing

other (please specify)
....

b Which waste do *you* separate for recycling?
c What do you do with your waste?
d What help does your local council provide?
e How could it help more?

Reading: a local campaign

2 Read about one of Intra's current projects. Then summarise in your own words what the project involves.

BEFORE Julia Edlund joined Intra, she worked as a sales and marketing consultant for a national newspaper. Now she is one of Intra's project leaders. She is responsible for particular clients, works to a budget and draws up marketing strategies.

One of her clients is Uppsala Council. The project is a four-year recycling campaign. The Council hopes that both behaviour and attitudes to recycling will be changed during the campaign; there is, for example, a totally false belief that the Council is not recycling all the waste it collects.

To begin with, the inhabitants of Uppsala will receive a starter pack containing a handbook that explains what common waste products are actually made from. They will also receive labels for their own personal bins at home. Larger bins for different kinds of waste will be provided outside by the council, and there will be public events to raise awareness of individual responsibilities.

114

Vocabulary: projects

3 Explain the meaning of these expressions from the text. Use a dictionary to help you.

*works to a budget   draws up marketing strategies
behaviour and attitudes   a starter pack
to raise awareness of individual responsibilities*

Grammar: *-ing* forms

4 Look at these phrases from the text. In which phrase is *recycling* used as a verb?

*a four-year recycling campaign
attitudes to recycling
the Council is not recycling all the waste*

5 Compare the uses of the word *walking* in A – F.
- A He's walking to work.
- B Walking is good for you.
- C Where's her walking stick?
- D I enjoy walking.
- E She's out, walking to the shops.
- F She's keen on walking.

a In which sentences can we replace *walking* by a noun (*a walk* or *walks*)?

b In which sentence is *walking* used as an adjective, before a noun?

c In which sentences is *walking* a verb form?

6 Practise using *-ing* forms.

a Complete these definitions. Use a dictionary to help you.
- Composting is *making* ...
- Recycling is ...
- Polluting means ...

b Complete these sentences about yourself. Use an *-ing* form after the preposition.
- I'm good at ...
- I'm looking forward to ...
- I'm thinking of ...

c Complete these sentences about yourself. Each verb is followed by an *-ing* form.
- I dislike ...
- I'm trying to give up ...
- I've always regretted ...

d Add a noun to these phrases, where the *-ing* form is used as an adjective.
- a boring ...
- a surprising ...
- a tiring ...

▶▶ p.117 **Grammar backup 14**

Speaking: discussing proposals

7 Imagine that your local council – or national government – has decided on strict measures to protect the environment.

a Add to this list of possible regulations:
- No household can own more than one car.
- Householders must compost all garden waste.
- All use of air-conditioning systems is forbidden.

b Give your list to a partner. Discuss both sets of proposals, using phrases from the *Phrasebook*. Which proposals do you both think could work?

Phrasebook

Accepting proposals

People won't mind compos**ting** garden waste.
I don't object to walk**ing** to work.
It's worth controll**ing** the use of central heating.

Rejecting proposals

It's not worth ask**ing** people to give up their cars.
There's no point in forc**ing** people to change their lifestyles.
We can't risk los**ing** voters **by** mak**ing** demands.

Word file   Unit 14

THE ENVIRONMENT
alternative *adj*
chemical *n*
compost *v*
electricity *n*
energy *n*
environmental concerns *n pl*
environmentally-friendly *adj*
green *adj*
harmful *adj*
poisonous *adj*
polluted *adj*
raw material *n*
recyclable *adj*
recycle *v*
renewable *adj*
resources *n pl*
reusable *adj*
safe *adj*
toxic *adj*
waste *n*
waste disposal *n*
wasteful *adj*

BUSINESS PLANS
agenda *n*
calculate *v*
consultant *n*
finances *n pl*
goal *n*
hire *v*
minutes *n pl*
implementation *n*
object *v*
policy *n*
proposal *n*
propose *v*
risk *v*

OTHER WORDS
air-conditioning *n*
attitude *n*
awareness *n*
bin *n*
council *n*
handbook *n*
input *n*
news-sheet *n*
output *n*
polystyrene *n*
starter pack *n*
work practices *n pl*

Grammar backup 14

Future perfect

Practice

1 Write complete sentences using the future perfect.

a I might / look at your proposal / tomorrow afternoon.
 I might have looked at your proposal by tomorrow afternoon.
b When will you / finish / writing that urgent report? By tomorrow, I hope.
c They won't / finish / their meeting / an hour's time.
d Everyone will / learn / how to use a computer / twenty years' time.

2 Look at the list of what Carol has to do this week. Write seven sentences (a – g) about what she will / won't / might have done by the end of today.

Things to do this week	Today
a phone the consultant	✓
b type the minutes	✓
c draw up the agenda	✓
d find the latest proposal	?
e calculate the budget	?
f send out the news-sheet	✗
g put together a starter pack	✗

a She will have phoned the consultant.

3 Complete the sentences about yourself using the future perfect.

a ..... by this time tomorrow.
b ..... by next weekend.
c ..... in a year's time.
d ..... in five years' time.

4 Translation

Write these sentences in your own language. Then close your Course Book. Translate the sentences back into English.

a Will people have become more environmentally friendly in 10 years' time?
b I might have changed my job by this time next year.
c He won't have finished his studies by June.

Reference

- We use the future perfect to talk about actions or situations that will be completed before a certain time in the future: *I'll have finished* this report **by** *tonight.*

  Now
  |
  12.00   18.00

- Time expressions that are most commonly used with future perfect verb forms are *by* and *in*: They **won't have read** all the questionnaires **by** this time tomorrow. **Will** you **have received** your results **in** a month's time?

- We form the future perfect with *will* + *have* + past participle. We often use contracted forms in spoken English: *I'll have* (aɪləv) *left for a meeting by the time you arrive. He* **won't have** (wəʊntəv) *read the consultant's report when we meet.*

- We can use *may* or *might* instead of *will* if we are less certain that the action will be completed: *We* **won't** *have finished the news-sheet by tomorrow.* (certain) *We* **might** / **may** *not have finished the news-sheet by tomorrow.* (not certain)

-ing forms

Practice

1 Complete the gaps with the infinitive or -ing form of the verb in brackets.

a Have you read Stuart's report? It's very *interesting* (interest)
b ..... (spend) too much time in front of a computer screen is bad for your eyesight.
c He's really looking forward to ..... (visit) Paris next month.
d I want ..... (see) you in my office.
e I'm thinking of ..... (apply) for the job at Mansfields. What do you think?
f They're ..... (give) their presentation at the conference.
g She's hoping ..... (go) on holiday next month.
h He used to ..... (travel) abroad on business but now he only covers the UK.

2 Correct the mistakes.

              hearing
a I look forward to ~~hear~~ from you in the near future.
b Don't worry. They're used to work late if they have to.
c If you have to speaking in a foreign language for a long time, it can be very tiring.
d I can go to the meeting if you're feel ill.
e I really don't like spend so much money on a new computer system.
f They enjoy to go to the cinema at the weekends.
g Three of my colleagues are French-spoken.
h I'd like proposing a compromise.
i Here's the file contain all the papers.

3 Translation
Write these sentences in your own language. Then close your Course Book. Translate the sentences back into English.

a I don't like spending money.
b Recycling waste is very important for the environment.
c I regret not studying harder at school.

Reference

- *-ing* forms can be used as adjectives: *a* **welcoming** *receptionist; an* **interesting** *idea*. They sometimes form part of compound nouns: *a* **washing** *machine*.
- They are used in continuous verb forms: *They're* **proposing** *to change the agenda. He's been* **working** *very hard*.
- They can show that two actions are happening at the same time: *He's in the office* **talking** *to Paul*.
- A clause with an *-ing* form can be used instead of a relative clause: *Here's the report* **containing** *(which contains) the latest figures*.
- *-ing* forms follow certain verbs: *I* **hate getting** *up early. He actually* **enjoys word-processing**.
- *-ing* forms can be the subject of a verb, or part of the subject: **Advertising** *is always necessary.* **Using** *public transport is better for the environment*.
- Like nouns, *-ing* forms follow prepositions: *Thank you* **for coming**. *I'm thinking* **of leaving**. Note that *to* is only followed by an *-ing* form (or a noun) when it is a preposition: *I'm looking forward* **to hearing** *from you*. At other times *to* is part of an infinitive verb form: *I want* **to go**.
- We use *used to* + infinitive to describe past situations that have changed . We use *used to* + *-ing* to describe a familiar situation: *I* **used to work** *for an American company* (but I don't now). *I'***m used to living** *in London now, but I found it strange at first*.

Services
The information age

15

Action A — Information overload?

- Listen to an interview
- Read a newspaper report
- Talk about information overload
- Vocabulary:
  suffixes
- Grammar:
  articles *a*, *an*, *the*,
  no article (Ø)

Listening to an interview

1 Jacob Bergström is a graphic designer who works at Intra. Listen. In what ways does he use the Internet as a 'tool'?

Reading a newspaper report

2 Not everyone is so relaxed about new technology. Look at the newspaper report below.

a What does the picture suggest that the report is about?

b What do you think these phrases from the report mean? Use a dictionary to help you.
- *the explosion in electronic communications*
- *information overload*
- *information fatigue syndrome*
- *The Information Age*
- *computer rage*

3 Now read the report.

a Check your answers to Exercise 2.
b What does the headline of the report refer to?
c How do you feel if you have *information fatigue syndrome*?
d What causes the problem?

FEATURE

Trying to climb a ladder under Niagara Falls

DO YOU EVER FEEL that it is all too much and that you are in danger of being swallowed by your computer? Are you unable to cope with the quantity of data produced by the explosion in electronic communication? Are you drowning in messages received via e-mail, the Internet, faxes and voice-mail? If so, you are experiencing information overload, and you may be suffering from *information fatigue syndrome*.

Before we can solve a problem or make a decision, we have to search through ever-expanding mountains of information; much of this information may be out of date, contradictory or inappropriate. Twenty years ago we only had to deal with communication by telephone, letter and telex. Information age workers have to answer dozens of e-mails, read piles of faxes and respond to calls on voice-mail, answering machines and mobile phones. The biggest fear of employees is that they cannot deal with all the information that arrives on their desk in the time available. One worker described the feeling as trying to climb a ladder under Niagara Falls!

The first signs of information fatigue syndrome are forgetfulness, headaches, bad temper, loss of concentration, sleep disturbance and anxiety. This can lead to computer 'rage' and often results in people literally hitting their PCs!

Vocabulary: suffixes

4 Look at the charts below.

a Find words in the report to complete the chart. Check the meanings of words that are new to you.

VERB	NOUN	ADJECTIVE
explode		explosive
communicate		communicative
forget		forgetful
disturb		
concentrate		

b Complete these statements about parts of speech.
- Words ending in *-ness*, *-ance* and *-ion* are often …
- Words ending in *-ful* and *-ive* are often …

c Now complete the chart below.

VERB	NOUN	ADJECTIVE
persuade		
operate		
		thoughtful
accept		
create		creative

d Do you know words that will fill any of the shaded boxes in the two charts?

Grammar: articles – *a*, *an*, *the* and no article (Ø)

5 Look at these sentences from the report.

a Study the box on the right, above. Choose an explanation (a – e) from the box for each of the uses of the article (1 – 11) in these sentences from the report.
- *Are you unable to cope with **the**[1] quantity of **(Ø)**[2] data produced by **the**[3] explosion in **(Ø)**[4] electronic communication?*
- *Before we can solve **a**[5] problem or make **a**[6] decision, we have to search through ever-expanding mountains of information …*
- ***(Ø)**[7] Information age workers have to answer dozens of e-mails … **The**[8] biggest fear for **(Ø)**[9] employees is that they cannot deal with all **the**[10] information that arrives on their desk in **the**[11] time available.*

b Translate the sentences from the report into your language. Do you use articles in the same ways?

We use:

THE before a noun that:
a is specific.
   the office on the corner
b refers to something of which there is only one.
   the sun

A / AN before a singular, countable noun that:
c is used as an example of all things of that kind.
   a computer saves time

NO ARTICLE (Ø) before a noun that:
d is plural and refers to all things of that kind.
   employers, teachers
e is uncountable and used in a general sense.
   poverty is everywhere

6 Complete this text with articles *a*, *an*, *the*, or Ø.

What would we do without (a) ….. computer that sits on our desk at work? It gives us access to an endless supply of information and allows us instant communication with people all over (b) ….. world. A number of (c) ….. people are questioning the value of (d) ….. huge amount of (e) ….. data that is now available via computers. 'These days (f) ….. companies are data-rich but information-poor,' says George Jones, (g) ….. financial manager from London. There is certainly a need for (h) ….. information policy and (i) ….. information director within (j) ….. large organisations. (k) ….. people need (l) ….. advice on how to deal with too much data.

▶▶ p.124 Grammar backup 15

Speaking: information overload

7 Work in pairs. Discuss the problem of information overload in relation to your own working or personal lives. Is it a problem for you? If so, what strategies do you use to deal with it?

Services

Action B

- Read and prioritise correspondence
- Write responses
- Vocabulary: collocations

Priorities

Reading and Speaking: prioritising correspondence

1 Work in pairs. The correspondence on these two pages has arrived on the desk of Charlotte Spender's assistant, Kathy. Read it and decide what Kathy should do with it.

a Which require immediate action? What action does Kathy need to take?
b Which require non-urgent action? What action does Kathy need to take?
c Which can Kathy throw in the bin? Why?

Vocabulary: collocations

2 These verbs and nouns often go together. Find another noun in the correspondence that goes with each verb.

a to confirm ... *an appointment*
b to hold ... *a conference*
c to pay ... *a bill*
d to win ... *a contract*
e to fill in ... *a visitor's book*
f to arrange ... *a meeting*
g provide ... *a meal*

Writing responses

3 Imagine you are Kathy. Decide which pieces of correspondence need a written response. Write the replies.

A

FAX

To: Charlotte
From: Jim
Date: May 27th
Pages: 1 (including this one)

Subject: Committee Meeting, May 29th.

Just a short note to confirm the arrangements for the next committee meeting. It will be held in my office on June 4th at 10.30am. You said you would bring five copies of your report.

See you then.

Jim

B

MESSAGE

To: Kathy   From: Charlotte
Date: 27/5   Time: 5.30 pm

Please call Mr Terry on 0181 009 6653 urgently about the missing order. He'll be in his office between 9 and 10am tomorrow.

C

INVOICE   No 3510

To: Charlotte Spender
From: White Horse Printing
Date: May 27th

For	
2000 A4 brochures	
Total	£1250.00

Please pay this invoice within 30 days.

Unit 15B

D

INVOICE REMINDER   **URGENT**

No.	1762
To:	C Spender, Portman Computer Accessories, Oxford
From:	Global Travel, March House, High Street, Oxford
Date:	May 27
For:	Plane tickets for K Jefferson London – Stockholm – London
Total	£638.00

Please note that this invoice was due for payment by May 15th. We would be grateful for full settlement immediately.

E

Dear Ms Spender

Your lucky number is 952749

You have <u>already</u> won a prize in our national competition. Just return this form and we will send you a RADIO ALARM CLOCK absolutely free! You may also have won our top prize of a

DREAM HOLIDAY IN THE CARIBBEAN!!

To find out, just fill in the form and send us the lucky number printed at the top of this letter.

F

0171 112 2877   28 MAY

FAX

To: Ms Spender
From: Mr L James
Date: May 28th
Pages: 1 (including this one)

Re: Computer maintenance contract 8775

Thank you for your payment relating to the above contract. I will call you in a few days to arrange our first visit to your offices.

Yours sincerely

Leonard James

Leonard James (Technical Director)

G

Message

To: Kathy
From: Charlotte   Date: May 27th

Patrick Jones of Mailfast is interested in some of our new products. Could you fax his secretary, Sarah Smith (01654 323187), and arrange a meeting here for some time next week? Thanks.

H

Dear Ms Spender

I enclose the minutes of last week's meeting of the European Business Association. The next meeting will be on August 17th at the Grosvenor Hotel in Victoria at 10am.

Yours sincerely

David Jones-Barrett

David Jones-Barrett

I

MEMO

To: All staff
From: Charlotte Spender
Date: May 28th

Please note that the ground floor offices will be closed for two weeks for building alterations from August 18th to 29th. Temporary accommodation will be provided on the second floor during that period.

Charlotte

J

From: Simon Williams, simon.williams@freeman.co
To: Charlotte Spender, charlspend@bignet.com
Date: 28/5/98   08:54
Re: Vienna

Thanks for message about John Taylor. I'll send the text on disk accompanied by paper copy.

Simon

121

Services

Action C

E-mail

- Talk about electronic mail
- Read and write e-mail messages
- End e-mail messages

Reading e-mail messages

1 Read the information on the computer screen below.

a How many messages are waiting?
b Who is the first message from?
c What is it about?
d This is how the first e-mail address is said:
leif at intra dot s e
Practise saying the other addresses.

Talking point

I CAN'T SEE THE POINT OF E-MAIL MESSAGES WHEN WE'VE GOT A FAX MACHINE.

YOU HAVE 27 MESSAGES

What do *you* think?

Get New Mail

Subject	Address
Intra information	leif@intra.se
Special offer	flo@perry.uk
New ads	timsmith@superpic.co.uk

2 Read messages 1 and 2 opposite. Answer these questions.

a What is Andy Snales' e-mail address?
b What is the purpose of each message?
c Which command (at the bottom of the screen) do you think Andy Snales used after he read message 1? What would have happened if he had used the other commands? Use a dictionary to help you.

3 The language contained in e-mail messages is often informal, and more like spoken language than a letter. Read messages 1 – 3. Find examples of:

a greetings   b short forms (grammar and vocabulary)   c endings

4 Look at message 4.

a Is this language informal? Why (not)?
b How does the message end?
c Are there any differences between this e-mail and a fax message?

Phrasebook

Endings in e-mail messages

FORMAL	FOR ANY E-MAIL	INFORMAL / CHATTY
Yours sincerely	Best wishes	See you
Yours truly	Best regards	All the best
Yours faithfully	Regards	Best
	Yours	Bye for now

122

Unit **15C**

1
Subject: Intra information
FROM: Leif Nordlund, INTERNET:leif@intra.se
TO: Andy Snales, snales@compuserve.com
DATE: 27/5/98 09:21
Re: Intra information

Hi! We'll send it all today, Thursday. You'll have it tomorrow, I hope.

Best Regards/Leif.   leif@intra.se

Intra Kommunikation – Salagatan 16, Box 3015 750 03 Uppsala, Sweden

Tel 018-56 30 00 – Fax 018-56 40 10 – http://www.intra.se

[In-basket] [File it] [Reply] [Forward] [Delete] [Cancel]

3
TO: Hotel des Beaux Arts, beauxarts@franconet.com
FROM: Alan Janiurek, janiurek@bignet.com
DATE: 27/5/98   21.14
Re: Reservation

Do you have a double room with bath for 2 nights - June 21/22? If so, please let me know the room rate. Is a no smoking room available? Also need to know if you have a car park.

janiurek@bignet.com
Tel: +44 1666 33001   Fax: +44 1666 33002

[In-basket] [File it] [Reply] [Forward] [Delete] [Cancel]

2
TO: Leif Nordlund, INTERNET:leif@intra.se
FROM: Andy Snales, snales@compuserve.com
DATE: 29/5/98 09:06
Re: Intra information

Good morning! Everything has arrived safely. The photos look really good and the background info will be very useful. Just one more thing. Have you got a list of the international companies you've worked with? I'd be grateful if you could e-mail it.

Oh yes, and have you got any info about organisations that monitor the environmental awareness of companies in the EU and US? That would be really helpful.

Thanks again for your help.

All the best, Andy

[In-basket] [File it] [Reply] [Forward] [Delete] [Cancel]

4
TO: Mr Alan Janiurek, janiurek@bignet.com   4
FROM: Hotel des Beaux Arts, beauxarts@franconet.com
DATE: 28/5/98 0   9.14
Re: Reservation/June 21-22

Thank you for your enquiry. I'm afraid the hotel is fully booked for the nights of June 21-22. Please let me know if we can be of help on any other occasion.

Yours sincerely

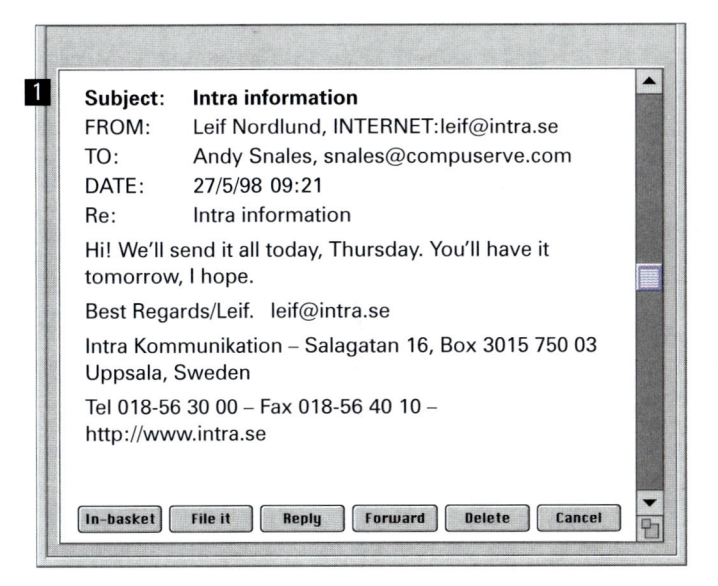

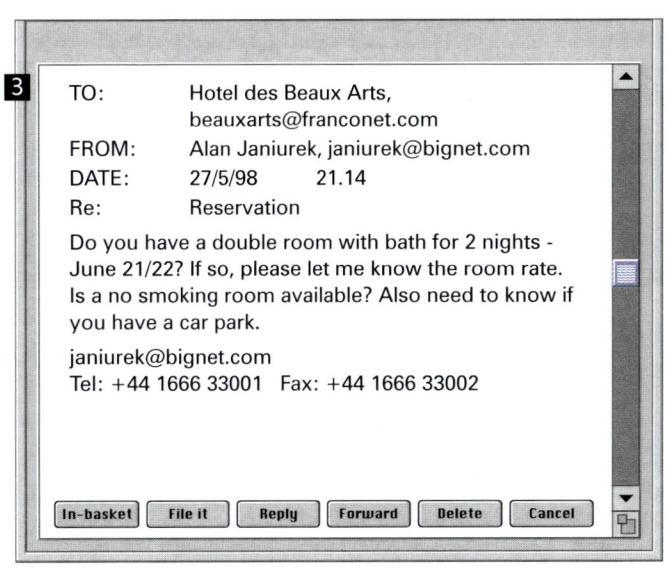

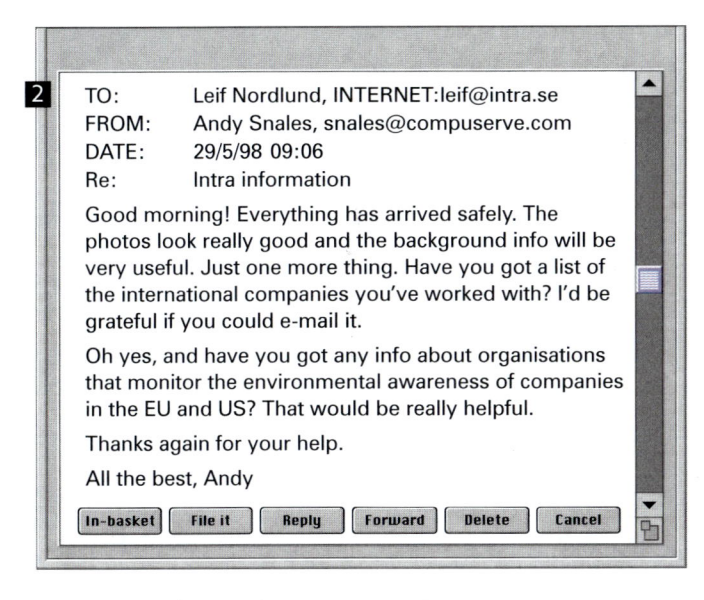

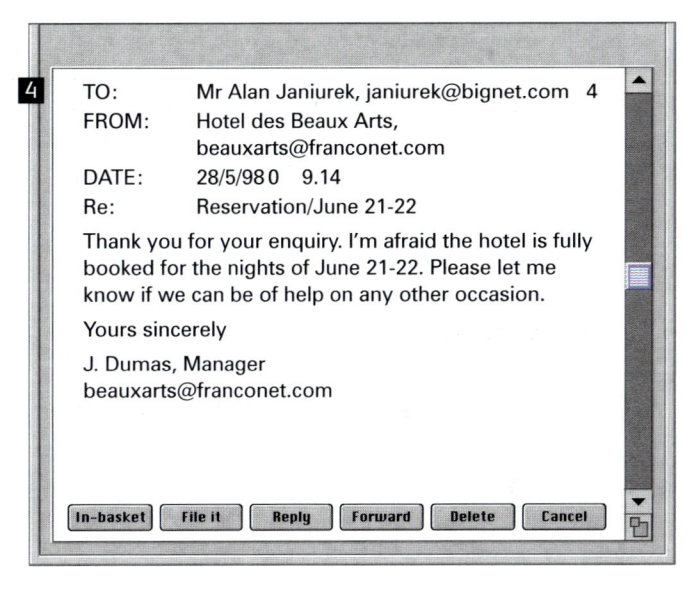

J. Dumas, Manager
beauxarts@franconet.com

[In-basket] [File it] [Reply] [Forward] [Delete] [Cancel]

Writing e-mail messages

5 Write e-mail messages for the situations below. Choose an appropriate way to end from the *Phrasebook* opposite.

a Imagine that you are Leif Nordlund. Write an e-mail reply to Andy Snales. Say that your secretary will post the things he has asked for – because there is too much to fax.

b Imagine that you work at the Hotel des Beaux Arts. Write a different reply to Alan Janiurek's e-mail. Use this information: double room available; no 'no smoking' rooms; free car park; room rate 600 francs excl. breakfast. Ask if he wants a reservation (credit card number?).

Word file   Unit 15

INFORMATION
concentration n
contradictory adj
data n
delete v
disk n
explosion n
file n
mobile phone n
out of date adj
overload n
prioritise v
retrieve v

subject n
voice-mail n

STRESS
anxiety n
bad temper n
cope v
disturbance n
fatigue n
forgetfulness n
headache n
rage n
syndrome n

OTHER
acceptance n
alteration n
creativity n
lucky adj
monitor v
operation n
persuasion n
persuasive adj
prize n
typeface n

123

Grammar backup 15

Articles *a*, *an*, *the*, no article (Ø)

Practice

1 Correct any mistakes in the use of articles in the text below.

> ~~A~~ **The** way we communicate has changed dramatically over past ten years. More and more people are beginning to use an e-mail in their working lives and the voice mail has been introduced into many offices as a way of helping people to communicate. And outside the work, the life has changed dramatically as well. The most people now own the answer machine and many carry the mobile phones. However, this is not always popular with the people around them: for example, in the UK, some railway companies have introduced carriages where no phones or laptop computers are allowed so passengers can enjoy the peaceful journey.

2 Complete the sentences using *a*, *an*, *the*, or no article (Ø).

a *(Ø)* information technology is developing all the time.
b Our company always has ..... large party in the summer for all its employees.
c She's ..... best friend I've ever had.
d Did you remember to bring ..... computer print-out I asked you for?
e A: I'd like to buy ..... new car this year.
   B: What happened to ..... old one you had?
f When I finish my studies, I want to be ..... advertising executive.
g Can you give me ..... advice about applying for a job?

3 Translation

Write these sentences in your own language. Then close your Course Book. Translate the sentences back into English.

a I need information about delivery dates.
b I need a holiday.
c Did you receive the fax I sent you last week?
d I've never eaten sushi.

Reference

- We use *a / an* with singular, countable nouns to refer to one of a class of things. No particular object is identified: *We need **a** new fax machine.*

- We use *a / an* when defining ourselves: *I work as **a** sales manager. I'm **a** music lover.*

- When we talk about things in general or a general concept, we use no article: *I like working with **figures**.* (all figures) ***E-mail** has revolutionised **international communication**. **Time** is **money**.* We can, though, use *a / an* and a singular noun to make a general statement.

- We use *the* with countable (singular and plural) and uncountable nouns to refer to something specific that our listener knows about or that we have already mentioned: *I gave you **the** report last week. Why don't you try **the** shops in the high street.*

- We also use *the* with superlative adjectives / adverbs or to refer to something of which there is only one: *It was **the** most expensive computer system on display. Let me pay **the** bill this time.*

Sound check

Intonation

Emphasising what's important

1 **Look at these sentences.**
   - 'Shall we get them a T-shirt each?'
     'John would like a T-shirt but I think Kate would prefer some chocolates.'
   - 'Oh, that's absolutely wonderful!'
   - 'Well I would prefer to go home now.'

a Underline the words that you think are stressed.
b Listen and compare your predictions. Explain why these words are stressed.
c Practise saying the sentences above.

2 **Practise this conversation with appropriate stress. Then listen and check.**

   A: 'Can I help you?'
   B: 'Yes. Do you sell children's clothes?'
   A: 'No, I'm afraid we only sell clothes for adults.'

Rising and falling intonation

1 **Listen to this sentence spoken in three ways.**

   The factory's near Moscow ...

a Which sentence (A, B or C):
   - is a question?
   - is a complete statement (the speaker has probably finished)?
   - is an incomplete statement (the speaker is probably going to continue)?

b Check your answers against these general rules.
   - Rising intonation often suggests a question.
   - Falling intonation often suggests that the speaker has finished speaking.
   - Fall-rise intonation often suggests that the speaker intends to continue.

2 **Listen to this conversation. What happens to the speaker's intonation at the end of each phrase? Complete the gaps with ↗, ↘ or ↘↗ .**

   A: I'm going to visit that company in Paris (.....)
   B: You are (.....)
   A: The boss wants me to collect some things (.....)
   B: Things (.....)
   A: You know, some brochures (.....), a few samples (.....) and he wants a price list (.....)

Services
Under pressure

16

Action A

- Talk about secretarial tasks and qualities
- Read a survey extract
- Listen to a secretary
- Discuss doing personal tasks
- Vocabulary: secretarial tasks and qualities

The ideal secretary

Speaking: secretarial tasks and qualities

1 **Look at the cartoon below. Work with a dictionary.**

a What is the name of the company?
b Why is the boss called Mr *Smug*?
c What is a *forthcoming crisis*?

2 **Discuss these questions.**

a Do you think the secretary is satisfied with her job? Why (not)?
b What general point do you think the cartoonist is making about secretaries and bosses? Do you agree / disagree?
c What tasks does the cartoonist show the secretary doing?
d What qualities does the cartoonist think a good secretary needs?
e Work with your partner and make lists. What other tasks does a secretary do? What other qualities does a good secretary need?

Vocabulary: the ideal secretary

3 **Choose the best meaning for these words from the survey and the comments on the opposite page. Use a dictionary to help you.**

a *common sense*: ~~a good education~~ / practical understanding and judgement
b *defuse*: make (a difficult situation) worse / make (a difficult situation) better
c *incoming mail*: mail going out of the office / mail coming into the office
d *screened*: recorded / answered by a secretary
e *accuracy*: ability to work fast / ability to do things correctly
f *confidentiality*: ability to keep information private / ability to act with confidence
g *shorthand*: manual work / a method of notetaking

Reading: a survey extract

4 Read the survey results below based on 100 male and 100 female British bosses and the comments in the speech bubbles.

a Compare your lists from Exercise 2e with the survey results and comments.

b Would any of the results or comments be different in your own country, or at your own place of work, do you think?

SURVEY

WHAT DO YOU WANT FROM YOUR SECRETARY?

What are the most important qualities of a secretary?

1	Efficiency and accuracy	76%	6	Understanding my business	27%
2	Initiative	50%	7	Interpersonal skills	24%
3	Confidentiality	42%	8	Team player	13%
4	Computer and office skills	31%	9	Other	2%
5	Flexibility	31%			

Are shorthand, computer skills and a willingness to do some personal tasks important?

	VERY IMPORTANT	IMPORTANT	NOT IMPORTANT
Shorthand	9%	29%	62%
Computer skills	81%	18%	15%
Personal tasks	12%	30%	57%

Do you prefer secretaries with a degree? Yes 20% No 80%

Would you employ a male secretary? Yes 67% No 33%

Would you prefer a bilingual secretary? Yes 39% No 61%

> ❝ I expect every one of my phone calls to be screened, even internal calls. If someone is trying to sell me financial services, she will make the necessary excuses. I also expect her to open my incoming mail, unless it is strictly confidential. I get nearly an inch of junk mail every day. ❞

> ❝ A good secretary has a lot of common sense, an excellent memory, the ability to defuse difficult situations, flexibility and good interpersonal skills. ❞

> ❝ My secretary's main job is to organise me and my time. He looks after my diary, makes sure that meetings and travel are arranged. If a lot of people want to see me, he decides what the priorities are. ❞

Talking point

What do *you* think?

Listening and Speaking: personal tasks

5 Listen to a secretary talking about the personal tasks she will and will not do for her boss.

a Make lists under these headings:
- Will do
- Won't do

b What reasons does she give for refusing to do certain tasks?

6 Work in pairs. If you were a secretary, would you do these tasks? Give reasons why you would / would not. Does it depend on the situation?

a Make coffee and water plants.
b Select and send a birthday present to the boss's wife / husband.
c Look after the boss's young children.
d Look after an important client's family.
e Collect the boss's clothes from the cleaners.

Services

Action B | Customer service

- Talk about dealing with customer services
- Listen to a staff trainer
- Listen to a difficult customer
- Discuss personal experiences
- Vocabulary: qualities and attitudes
- Grammar: should have (done)

Speaking: customer services

1 Some administrative staff work in Customer Services Departments. What is the purpose of these departments? Why do people contact them?

Vocabulary: qualities and attitudes

2 The person in the pictures below works in the Customer Services Department of a large company.

a Which picture do you think gives the right impression to customers? Give reasons.
b What is wrong with the others?
c Use the words below and others you know to describe how the person looks in each of the pictures.

hostile	threatening	aggressive	concerned	(un)interested
(un)friendly	(un)welcoming	(un)professional	defensive
warm	(in)attentive	(in)sincere	(un)pleasant	(un)friendly
cold	(un)helpful	well-organised	disorganised	(in)efficient

128

Unit 16B

Listening and Writing: dealing with difficult customers

3 A staff trainer describes some difficult customers and how to deal with them. What do you expect her to say? Answer the questions. Then listen and compare your answers with the trainer's comments.

a What is the main aim of staff in Customer Services?
b What types of difficult customer are there?
c How should we deal with these people?

Listening: a difficult customer

4 Listen to a conversation. A customer is talking to a Customer Services assistant. Answer these questions.

a What is the problem?
b How does the customer feel at the beginning of the conversation? Are her feelings justified? Why (not)?
c How does she feel at the end of this extract? Are her feelings justified? Why (not)?
d How does the assistant respond to the woman's behaviour?
e How would you describe the assistant's behaviour?
f How do you think the conversation will end?
g What do you think the customer's opinion of the company will be?

Grammar: should have (done)

5 The situation in Exercise 4 is clearly unsatisfactory. Look at the trainer's comments below and answer the questions.

'The company should have sent an engineer to the woman's home.'
'If there was a problem, they should have told her.'

a Did the company send an engineer?
b Did they tell the customer that there was a problem?
c Did the company behave well?
d What part of speech follows *should have*?
e When do we use this construction?

6 Listen to the conversation again. Make notes on these points.

a What was the Customer Services assistant doing wrong? What should he have said and done to make the conversation more successful? What shouldn't he have said and done?
   EXAMPLE: *He should have listened calmly to the woman's problem.*

b The customer made mistakes too. What should she have said and done to make her complaint more effective?

▶▶ p.132 **Grammar backup 16**

Speaking: personal experiences

7 Discuss situations in which you have provided or contacted customer services. How successful were the transactions? Why, do you think?

129

Services

Action C — Telephone complaints

- Talk and read about complaints
- Listen to a complaint and complete a form
- Make and deal with a complaint
- Grammar:
  can't have / must have / might have (done)

Speaking: complaints

1 What might people complain about in these particular business settings? Make lists.

A clothes shop:	Bad service, ...
A camera manufacturer:	...
A television company:	...
An advertising company:	...

Reading: handling complaints

2 Staff trainers identify seven stages for handling a complaint.
  a Match the stages on the left with the explanations on the right.
  b Put the stages in a sensible order.

SYMPATHISE	a) Let the caller explain the problem.
CHECK	b) Summarise the caller's complaint.
LISTEN	c) Apologise personally on behalf of the company.
CLARIFY	d) Make the caller realise you understand their point of view.
TAKE RESPONSIBILITY	e) Find out the facts. Often these are available on a computer.
ANSWER / RESPOND	f) End the call with a final apology and a promise.
SIGN OFF	g) Suggest positive action.

Listening to a telephone complaint

3 Listen to the conversation.
  a Complete the complaint form with information from the conversation.
  b Listen to the whole conversation again. Listen for the phrases in the *Phrasebook* and match them with the stages in Exercise 2. Do they follow the order that you predicted?

Phrasebook

Handling a complaint

Could you tell me exactly what the problem is?
I understand how you feel.
So the problem is that your photocopier is not working ... ?
Could you give me the order details, please?
I apologise. This does seem to be our fault.
I'll see what I can do.
I'll arrange for a technician to come to you immediately.
Let me apologise once again.

COMPLAINT FORM

Date: *March 8th*
Time: *10.10 am*
Taken by: ....

Name of person complaining: ....
Position: ....
Company ....
Address: ....
Telephone number: ....

Complaint: ....
....

Action promised: ....
....

130

Grammar: *can't have (done)*, *must have (done)*, *might have (done)*

4 Look at these sentences from the telephone conversation.

Caller: *It can't have been out of stock!*
Secretary: *Someone here must have made a mistake.*

a How sure is the caller that the part was in stock?
b What evidence does he have for his belief?
c How sure is the secretary that the part was *not* in stock?
d What evidence does *she* have?
e How are the verb structures formed in these sentences?
f Explain the meaning of this sentence in your own words.
The maintenance man might have spoken to the wrong person.

5 Look at a secretary's diary on the right and the comments by telephone callers. Are the callers correct? Use *can't have / must have / might have* in your answers to the callers.

a 'I can't remember when I met him — it was at a party.' (Jo Jackson)
You must have met him on Monday, Miss Jackson. That was the Staff Party.
b 'I visited your Service Department last Friday.' (Ted Porter)
c 'I'm sure you ordered the wine for the 7th.' (Alan Simpson)
d 'Your Managing Director agreed when I met him here last Wednesday.' (Jane Wills)
e 'I spoke to your new Customer Services manager on Monday.' (Sara Francis)
f 'We tried to deliver the parcel on Thursday morning but there was nobody around.' (Bill Jenkins)

▶▶ p.133 **Grammar backup 16**

Speaking: a telephone complaint

6 Work in pairs. Have a telephone conversation. Then change roles.

A: Read the information in the box. You are phoning to complain and you are angry. Use your own name and make up a name, address and telephone number for your company.

> You ordered a new business telephone line one month ago. The sales department of the telephone company promised you it would be installed within three weeks. Until the new line is installed you are losing business. Complain about the delay and find out what is happening.

B: You work in Customer Relations and receive a complaint from A. Complete a complaint form like the one opposite and deal with A's complaint. Follow the stages from Exercise 2 and use expressions from the *Phrasebook* to help you.

---

6 Monday
6pm Staff Party

7 Tuesday
New Customer Services manager starts work.

8 Wednesday
MD away (Glasgow)

9 Thursday
Receptionist away – George on reception all day.

10 Friday
PUBLIC HOLIDAY

11 Saturday

12 Sunday

Word file Unit 16

ATTITUDES
ag**gress**ive *adj*
(in)at**ten**tive *adj*
(un)con**cerned** *adj*
con**fused** *adj*
de**fen**sive *adj*
hostile *adj*
in**sult**ing *adj*
nervous *adj*
(un)pro**fess**ional *adj*
smug *adj*
(un)**threat**ening *adj*
(un)**wel**coming *adj*

QUALITIES
accuracy *n*
common **sense** *n*
confidenti**al**ity *n*
flexibility *n*
i**deal** *adj*
memory *n*
rudeness *n*
team player *n*

VERBS
clarify *v*
de**fuse** *v*
re**spond** *v*
sign **off** *v*
sort **out** *v*
sympathise *v*
threaten *v*

OTHER WORDS
crisis *n*
elderly *adj*
en**gaged** *adj*
evidence *n*
forthcoming *adj*
incoming *adj*
in**ter**nal *adj*
interper**son**al *adj*
junk mail *n*
liar *n*
maintenance *n*
on be**half** of
out of **stock**
servant *n*
shorthand *n*
spare part *n*
strictly *adv*

Unit **16C**

131

Grammar backup 16

should have (done)

Practice

1 You have received the letter below from Martin Goring. Complete your notes for your reply with *should / shouldn't have* + past participle.

a The sales department shouldn't have promised the wrong delivery date.
b The sales department ..... the photocopier within seven days.
c The receptionist ..... rude and unhelpful.
d The receptionist ..... polite and helpful.
e She ..... to take his name.
f I ..... him back immediately.

---

45 Castle Street
Stockton
Lancs L34 9RU

9 September

Dear Mr Ridgeway,
I am writing to complain about the service that I have received from your sales department.
 I ordered a new 756 photocopier and was promised that it would be delivered within seven days. That was three weeks ago! When I phoned your customer services department yesterday, the receptionist was very rude and unhelpful. She refused to take my name and then eventually she told me that she would ask you to phone me back. You never did!
 As you can imagine, I am very unhappy with the quality of service that I have received from your company. I have been a customer of yours for ten years and have never had cause to complain. I look forward to hearing from you.

Yours sincerely,

Martin Goring

Martin Goring
Freshwater Printing

---

2 Correct the mistakes.

a I should have not stayed up all night – I feel terrible!
b You ought have come last night. It was a good party.
c Should I have ask them again?
d I shouldn't has lost my temper with my boss.

Reference

- We use *should have* + past participle to talk about a past action or situation which did not happen. We often use it to be critical: *They **should have listened** to their customers' complaints.* (It was wrong that they didn't listen.) *We **shouldn't have eaten** so much last night.* (It wasn't a good idea that we ate so much.)

- We can also use *ought to have* + past participle in a positive statement but *should* is more usual. We usually use *should*, not *ought to*, in questions and negative statements: *I **ought to / should have returned** his phone call yesterday – it was rude not to. **Should** I have written to them?*

- We use contracted forms in spoken English: *He **shouldn't have** (ʃʊdəntəv) been so rude. We **should have** (ʃʊdəv) waited for his phone call.*

3 Translation
Write these sentences in your own language. Then close your Course Book. Translate the sentences back into English.

a They should have ordered more spare parts.
b He shouldn't have spent so much money.
c Should we have contacted them earlier?

can't have / must have / might have (done)

Practice

1 Complete the gaps with *must have*, *can't have*, or *might have* + past participle.

a We *must have met* (meet) before – I recognised her immediately I saw her.
b It ..... (be) very hot – they were wearing thick coats!
c We knocked on the door but he didn't hear us. He ..... (be) on the phone, or perhaps he wasn't there.
d She ..... (be) very unhelpful if Robert complained – he's usually so polite.
e Can you check the file? I think I ..... (write) to them already.

2 Write a sentence for each of these situations with *must have*, *can't have*, or *might have* + past participle.

a I had my bag on the bus. I haven't got it now.
  I must have left my bag on the bus.
b There was no message from the manager of Photocopier Express on the answerphone.
  He ..... .
c Did I order some more fax rolls? I can't remember.
  I ..... .
d They asked me a lot of questions in the meeting, but the answers were already in the report which I sent last week.
  They ..... .
e He left home 30 minutes late. I don't know if he caught the plane.
  He ..... .
f It's after 7 p.m. There's no answer from the sales department and the office is closed.
  All the staff ..... .
g I sent him an e-mail saying that I would be late but I don't know if he's read his mail today.
  He ..... .

Reference

- We use *must have* + past participle to make conclusions about past actions or situations which we believe are logically true. We use *can't have* + past participle (not *mustn't*) for past actions or situations which we believe are logically impossible: He **must have faxed** the report – here's the transmission slip. She **can't have travelled** by plane – she hates flying. Compare: He **faxed** the report. (You know because you saw him do it or he told you.) He **must have faxed** the report. (You have reason to believe he did it.)

- We use *might (not) have* + past participle if we believe that a past event possibly happened: We **might have met** last year in Paris – I can't remember. We can also use *may (not) have* and *could have* + past participle to express possibility. She **could have gone** directly to the meeting. She **may not have seen** my message.

- We use contracted forms in spoken English: She **must have** (mʌstəv) been furious when she heard the news. They **might have** (maɪtəv) called when we were out. We **can't have** (kɑːntəv) been here before – I'd remember.

3 Translation

Write these sentences in your own language. Then close your Course Book. Translate the sentences back into English.

a They can't have told me last week – I wasn't here!
b He must have known it was out of stock.
c He might have left early. It's his birthday.

133

Learning Skills

Using dictionaries 1

1 Look at the words below.

| advise | advice | advisory | advertisement | advisable | advertising |

a In what order do you think they appear in a dictionary?

b Look at the entries from the *Longman Active Study Dictionary* on the right. Check your answers.

2 Look at your own dictionary and the list (A–J) below.

a Which of these things can your dictionary do for you?
  A Tell you the meaning of a word.
  B Give an example of how we use a word.
  C Give you information about the grammar of a word.
  D Tell you how we say a word.
  E Tell you if we use a word in formal or informal English.
  F Tell you if a word is more common in American or British English.
  G Show you pictures of objects.
  H Tell you how we spell a word.
  I Give you help through exercises and study notes.
  J Give you a translation of the word in your language.

b Now look again at the entries from the *Longman Active Study Dictionary*. Which of the features (A–J) are there?

3 Look at the table below.

a Complete the first line using the dictionary entries.

Noun	Person	Verb	Adjective
		ad'vise	
		'analyse	
		ap'ply	
		repre'sent	

b Now complete the rest of the table. Do not worry if you do not know all the words.

c Use your dictionary to check your answers.

d Look at the example words given in the table. Note how the main stress is marked with a ' before the stressed syllable. Mark the main stresses on the other words in the same way.

---

ad·ver·tise /'ædvətaɪz ‖ -ər-/ v **advertised, advertising 1** [I;T] to tell the public about something, such as an event, service or article for sale, for example in a newspaper or on television: *I advertised my house in the "Daily News".* | *a poster advertising shampoo* **2** [I] to ask someone or something by placing a notice somewhere like a newspaper or shop window: *We should advertise* **for** *someone to look after the garden.* –**advertiser** n

ad·ver·tise·ment /əd'vɜːtɪsmənt ‖ ˌædvərˈtaɪz-/ n (also **ad, advert** *infml*) something used for advertising things, such as a notice on a wall or in a newspaper, or a short film shown on television

ad·ver·tis·ing /'ædvərtaɪzɪŋ ‖ -ər -/ n [U] the business of encouraging people to buy goods through advertisements

ad·vice /əd'vaɪs/ n [U] an opinion given by one person to another on how that other should behave or act: *I asked the doctor for her advice.* | *On her advice I am staying in bed.* | *Let me give you a piece of advice.*
▪ USAGE The word **advice** is uncountable and is not, therefore, used in the plural: *She gave me a lot of good* **advice**. | *Ask your teacher for* **advice**. | *a piece of excellent* **advice**

ad·vi·sab·le /əd'ævaɪzəbəl/ adj [never before a noun] sensible or wise: *It is advisable always to wear a safety belt when you're driving.* opposite **inadvisable** – **advisability** /əd'vaɪzəˈbɪləti/ n [U]

ad·vise /əd'vaɪz/ v **advised, advising 1** [T] to tell someone what you think they should do: *The doctor advised me to take more exercise.* | *I advised him that he should join a union.* | *Can you advise me where to stay?*
▪ USEFUL PATTERNS to advise someone; to advise someone to do something; to advise someone that they should do something; to advise someone how, where, when… etc.
2 advise against something, advise someone against something to warn someone not to do something: *Lawyers advised against signing the contract.* | *He advised me against giving up my job.*
3 [I;T] to act as a professional adviser to someone: *the experts who advise the President* | *She advises on legal matters.* **4** [T] *fml* to inform someone about something: *We wish to advise you that you now owe the bank £500.*

ad·vis·er /əd'vaɪzə ʳ/ n (also **advisor** *AmE*) a person whose job is to give advice, especially to a government or business: *the President's special adviser* on *foreign affairs*

ad·vi·so·ry /əd'vaɪzəri/ adj having the power or duty to advise people

134

Learning Skills

Using dictionaries 2

1. What information about the grammar of words do you expect to find in a dictionary?

2. Look at the words below and their grammar codes.

   careful *adj*   **age** *n*   **glance** *v* [I; + *adv/prep*]
   pay *n* [U]   **on** *adv, prep*   **look into sthg** *phr v* [T]

   a Which words are shown as:
   • nouns?   • verbs?   • adjectives?

   b Which noun can be countable?

   c Which verb is followed by an object?

   d What grammar codes does your own dictionary use?

3. Read this newspaper extract and answer the questions below.

   > THE <u>practice</u> of teleworking, or working for a company from home, is only just becoming popular in California. In Britain teleworking is more common. Some people in government and big businesses do not <u>view</u> it as a serious alternative to traditional working practices, though; it <u>sounds</u> nice but is too complicated to turn into an <u>official</u> policy. The main advantage of teleworking, of course, is that cars are <u>left</u> in the garage more often as workers sit at home in front of their computers with a modem connection to the office. <u>Staff</u> like it because their working hours become more flexible.

   a What part of speech is each underlined word (in this context)?

   b Find the words in your dictionary. Can the words be different parts of speech in different contexts? Are other meanings possible?

4. Check the meanings of the words *firm* and *form* in your dictionary. What do they mean in these sentences? What parts of speech are they?

   a That advertising firm has made large profits.
   b You need to be firm with young children.
   c I like to sleep on a firm bed.
   d I have a firm belief in the company's future success.
   e Can you fill in the form please?
   f They have formed a new political party.
   g Free samples are a form of promotion.
   h My younger son is in Mrs Trappe's form.

5. How do dictionaries deal with the different forms of words?

   a Look at these three dictionary entries from the *Longman Active Study Dictionary*. What parts of speech are the words? What do the entries tell you about the forms of the words?

   > **scarf** /skɑːf ‖ skɑːrf/ *n* **scarfs** or **scarves** /skɑːvz ‖ skɑːrvz/ a piece of cloth that you wear round your neck / head / or shoulders to keep warm or to look attractive

   > **sink**[1] /sɪŋk/ *v* **sank** /sæŋk/, **sunk** /sʌŋk/ **1** [I;T] to go down or make something go down below a surface /

   > **far**[1] /fɑːr/ *adv* **farther** /fɑːrðər ‖ fɑːr-/ *or* **further** /fɜːðər ‖ 'fɜːr-/, **farthest** /fɑːðɪst ‖ fɑːr-/ *or* **furthest** /fɜːðɪst ‖ 'fɜːr-/ **1** a long way away: *Is it far to your house:*

   b Find the word *tell* in your own dictionary. Does the dictionary give the past tense form and the past participle? What other grammatical information is given?

6. Work in pairs. Find the meanings of these words in your dictionary, and check their grammar. You have five minutes to make up a story, using all the words. Then tell your story to the rest of the class. Whose story is best?

   flashy   popcorn   dawn   haunt   recover

Learning Skills

Learning new words

1. Work in pairs. What does it mean to know a word? What information do you need about the word?

2. 🎧 Friederike is talking to her teacher.

a. Listen and make notes about how she learns new words.

b. What do you think of Friederike's system? What do you do?

3. It is important to record new words in a way that suits you. Look at the different ways below. How are the words organised?

A hill, mountain, windy, beach, sea

B firm, queue, income, escalator, wet, population, meeting point ....

C AT THE AIRPORT
- Check-in desk — show your passport
- leave your luggage — get your boarding card
- Exchange bureau: change money, buy traveller's cheques
- Departure Lounge: buy your duty free
- go to the gate — get on the plane

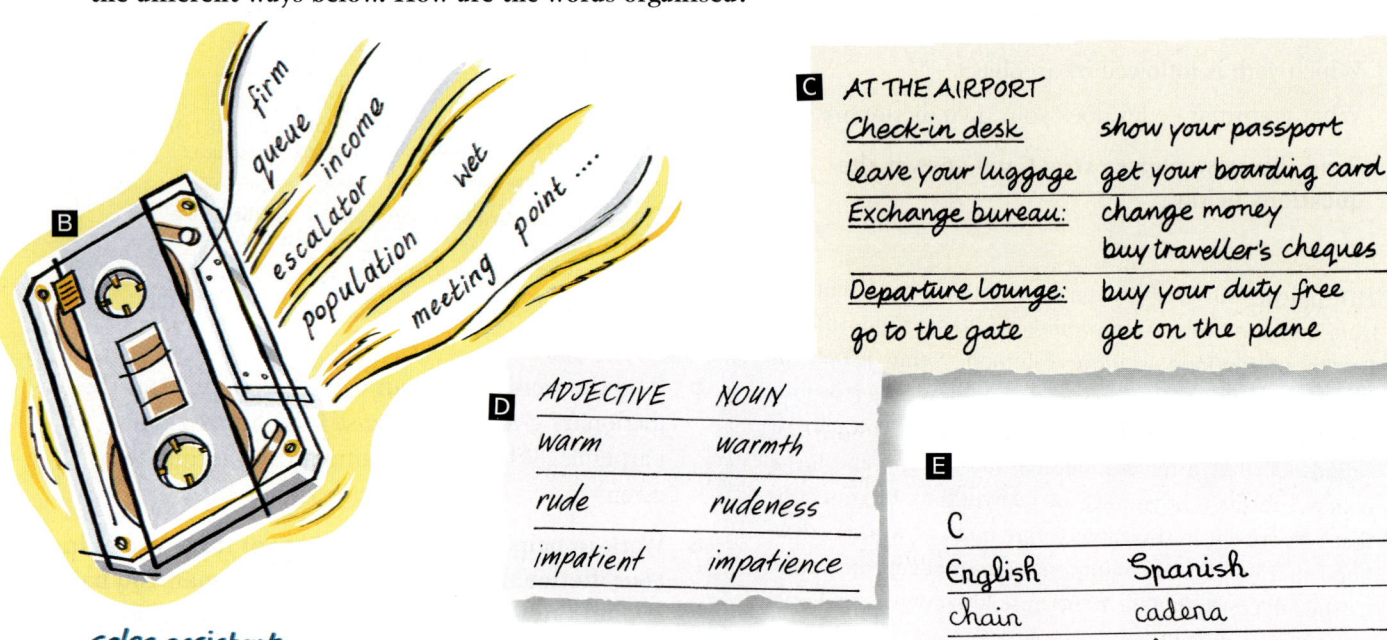

D
ADJECTIVE	NOUN
warm	warmth
rude	rudeness
impatient	impatience

E
C
English	Spanish
chain	cadena
climate	clima
charter flight	vuelo chárter
cash machine	cajero automático
car hire	alquiler de coches

F SHOPS
- People: sales assistant, deputy manager, manager
- Shops at airport or station: station bookshop, duty-free shop, airport shop
- Other kinds of shops: local shop, high street shop, newspaper stand, chemist's
- Other ways of buying things: mail order, street market, catalogue

G
- tourist / fishing | industry
- departures / arrivals | board
- airport / duty-free / high-street / local | shop
- airline / tourist | office

4. Work in pairs. Choose a Word file from any Course Book unit. How are the words organised? What other possibilities are there for those words?

5. How are you going to organise your vocabulary notebook? Which techniques are you going to try?

136

Learning Skills

Improving your English outside the classroom

1 Do you do anything outside the classroom to practise your English? If so, what?

2 Look at the list of ideas below. Write the main reason for doing each one.
   - Listening
   - Reading
   - Speaking
   - Writing
   - Grammar
   - Vocabulary

a Buy a vocabulary practice book and complete a unit each week. *Vocabulary*
b Organise a reading group at work and swap articles.
c Write a summary of an interesting article you have read. Give it to another colleague to read.
d Speak to a friend or colleague in English for 15 minutes every day.
e Organise a study group: meet regularly and do exercises together.
f Review new vocabulary once a week and get a colleague or friend to test you.
g Keep a diary in English. If you want, show it to your teacher or another learner.
h Watch a film or a video in English twice a month.
i When you read newspapers or magazines, look for examples of grammar that you have studied in class.
j Read short articles or conversations from *More Work in Progress* aloud and record them on a cassette recorder.
k Read an article in English twice a week.
l Find a 'cassette' colleague: record a cassette with news about yourself or what's happening at work and send it to him or her.

3 Think of ONE more thing you can do to practise each of the different areas.

4 Now choose TWO of the areas. Complete the study plan for the next two weeks. Remember to review it.

	Activity	Date done
Area 1		
Area 2		

137

Tapescripts

Introduction Exercise 2

1 So we can design your Web site for you, but we suggest that you also run a television campaign. You can have a great Web site, but it's no good if no one knows it's there. So one reason for the TV ads would be to promote the Web site – to encourage people to visit it.

2 A: Can I pay in pounds for these?
 B: Yes, certainly. Let me see. Er ... the paper's 300 pesetas, those are five-fifty, so that's eight hundred and fifty pesetas, please.

3 Of course it's mainly a music channel, and the news we present is young people's news. It's about 50% music news and 50% social – anything that interests people between 15 and 25.

4 In this part of the factory everything is hand-made. Some of our most famous chocolates are produced here.

Unit 1B Exercise 5

(Carmen)
A lot of our customers are British, of course – especially on Tuesdays and Saturdays when the charter flights come in. But we speak English in the shop with everyone except Spanish people. They come in to buy a newspaper or magazine for the plane. Some people are impatient or rude because they're in a hurry. Other people have a lot of time before they catch their plane, so they stop and chat. We can do that on quiet days – but on Saturdays there are long queues. Then some people come for help – they can't find a cash machine, or they want to know where Burger King is. They have all kinds of problems.

Unit 1C Exercise 2

(T = traveller, R = Raquel)
T: Can you help me, please? I must change my pesetas back into pounds before I leave.
R: Yes, well the exchange bureau is on this floor, but it's over there in the departure lounge. I'm afraid you can't change money until you go through the security check.
T: Oh, right. Thank you.

(T = traveller, N = Nuria)
T: Excuse me. I left my bag here somewhere and now I can't find it.
N: You needn't worry. The security guards have probably taken it. You should ask at the Lost and Found office. It's downstairs, on the ground floor. You can use the stairs, just there, or the escalators.
T: Oh, thanks a lot.

Unit 2A Exercises 2 and 3

(C = customer, N = Nuria)
C: I'd like this magazine, please.
N: Right. Are you paying in pounds?
C: No, pesetas. This one's six hundred pesetas, isn't it?
N: Let's see ... yes, that's right.
C: Here you are. A thousand.
N: Thanks. Here's your change.
C: Thank you.
N: Would you like a bag?
C: Yes, please. Thanks.
N: I've seen you before, haven't I? Do you live here?
C: Yes, we moved here last year.
N: Oh, right. See you again, then.
C: Yeah, bye.

Unit 2A Exercise 4

How much is it?
Are you paying in pounds?
This one's 600 pesetas, isn't it?
This one's 600 pesetas, isn't it?

Unit 2A Exercise 6

(N = Nuria, C = customer)
N: Hello. Can I help you?
C: Yes, I'd like this book, please, but I've only got pounds.
N: That's all right. We take pounds. What does the price tag say?
C: Er... one thousand one hundred pesetas.
N: One thousand one hundred. That's five pounds, please.

Unit 2B Exercise 5

(Andrew)
In the summer we have English books and English magazines next to each other. As you walk in through the main door you'll see English books and magazines, for the simple reason that the majority of our customers in that period are English. Now, in November, probably next week, we'll be looking to move it around so that the Spanish books and Spanish magazines are the ones that you see as soon as you go in the door, because the majority of the customers that you get between now and May next year are Spanish nationals. It's very seasonal.
We have the sweets right in front of the window, for the simple reason that you see it and it attracts the attention. It's bright, it's lit up, you've got all the Mars products on top so the children see it. If the parents get dragged in, the kid's going to have a sweet and the mum and dad might buy a magazine.
And we obviously put all the children's books etc. together, so we've got a Disney section which is right next to the children's books. The Disney section's bright and colourful, and it's got things from Pocahontas, from the Hunchback of Notre Dame, Toy Story, as well as Mickey Mouse, so nine times out of ten a young child will walk in through the door, see that, and they're immediately brought over there. Once they're over there, there's the books as well.
Behind the till we've got tobacco because it's more often than not an impulse purchase. We've got a chewing gum display unit next to the till, which we sell a lot, for the simple reason that people pick up a newspaper and as they're paying for it they'll just pick up a packet of chewing gum. And then behind the till as well we've got things like batteries and films, because if anyone's going to take anything out of our shop, batteries and films are quite high-risk areas.

Unit 2B Exercises 7 and 8

A: The trouble is that people are only buying the fresh meat. We're not selling anything at all from the freezer.
B: Shall we stop selling the frozen stuff, then?
A: No, I don't think that's the answer. Some people want frozen meat, so we need to have it there. I suppose we could move the freezer.
B: Yes, or replace it with one with a clear top, so customers can see what's in it.
A: Hey, that's a good idea. Right, let's buy a new freezer. And why don't we put up some signs to draw attention to the frozen meat?
B: Good idea. Oh, and have you thought about doing some special offers? Two for the price of one. Just for a week or so. It might help.
A: OK. Let's try.

Unit 2C Exercises 3 and 4

(D = Dave, S = Sue)
D: Oh, I'll buy some wine for Kevin. It's cheaper than in England. Look at those pots. Would Jane like one of those? Or a basket?
S: I don't think she'd like either of them much. Anyway they're difficult to carry home. Maybe a pair of these sandals.
D: Oh, yes, they're quite nice. In fact I think she'd love them. Now Tom ...
S: He'd be happy with a stuffed donkey, or a doll. That's fun, or one of those mugs. Which shall we get?
D: None of them. They're all awful. Completely tasteless.
S: So? He's only nine. Let's get him the doll. Now, who else? Your mother ...
D: She doesn't really need any of these things. Well, perhaps the tablecloth?
S: Yes, it's lovely. Or would she prefer something to eat – this ... um ... turrón?
D: No, look, it's got nuts in it. The tablecloth, then. Right, so what have we decided?

Unit 3C Exercise 1

(Isabel)
It is very important for sales staff to speak at least some English. The shop is in an international airport, and W H Smith is a British company, so customers expect it. If staff can say hello, talk about prices and give directions in English ... that's the minimum I need from them. Most of them speak much better English than that, though.
When I choose new staff, I also look at their experience, but they haven't all worked in shops before and of course we train them. They have to handle money and people confidently.
Personality is very important. Staff must be warm and open with customers and very patient and polite, even when people are being difficult. In quiet periods some customers want a chat while they wait for their plane, and that's fine. Some need help, so staff give a lot of information and advice which is not really part of the job.
They are normally expected to wear a red W H Smith T-shirt, so customers can identify them – that's the uniform. We're open seven days a week, from seven in the morning to ten at night – and to midnight sometimes in the summer if there are a lot of night flights – so we all work different hours, and the shifts are quite complicated. People need to be flexible. In fact we're only closed on three days a year, when there are no newspaper deliveries.

Tapescripts

Unit 3C Exercise 6

(Aileen)

Flower deliveries arrive from our wholesaler each Monday and Thursday morning. They come from all over the world, and many are imported from the international flower market in Amsterdam. Those two days start with three hectic hours cutting and preparing the flowers, and placing them in water in the cool, dark storeroom.

I've been here for over a year, learning the skills of floristry by working with the shop owner – but there is still a great deal to learn. It was at least six months before I felt confident enough to deal with the many different questions that customers ask. With ever-changing varieties of plants and flowers to find out about, I may never stop learning. Floristry involves far more than putting flowers in water. As well as looking after cut flowers and plants we have a workshop to make up bouquets and other displays, and I'm learning how to produce more complex arrangements. We also have a computer terminal for the Interflora orders. Shops throughout the world are linked to the system, and we send and receive many orders each day. Not all our customers visit us for happy reasons of course, and some come in soon after the death of a relative or close friend. That can sometimes be very distressing. I need to be sympathetic, and try to give them whatever advice they need.

Most people working in shops will tell you about those occasional customers who are difficult to serve or not very polite. This happens even in a flower shop, but I must say that meeting the vast majority of customers, both young and old, is the most enjoyable part of each working day.

Unit 4B Exercise 2

1 In green? Size 42? I'll just check for you.
2 Please have your passports and boarding passes ready for inspection.
3 Would Mr Pirelli, travelling to Rome on flight IB 487, please go immediately to Gate 16.
4 Can you open that green case, please? Thank you. So where have you just come from?
5 Did you pack your bags yourself? Good. And have they been with you at all times?
6 That's 550 pesetas for the coffees. Would you like anything else?
7 Right. Could you give me a detailed description of the bag and its contents. What colour is the suitcase?
8 Right. There are seats available at 2.00 and 4.30. When would you like to travel?
9 Yes, we do charge commission on traveller's cheques. Our rates are on the board here.
10 Would you mind moving away from the entrance, please?

Unit 4C Exercise 6

(A = cashier, B = customer)
A: Good morning. Can I help you?
B: I'd like to change some dollar traveller's cheques into pesetas, please.
A: Fine. How much would you like to change?
B: Er ... What's the rate for the dollar today?
A: It's 127 pesetas.
B: Right. I see. Um ... I'll just change a hundred dollars, then, please.
A: A hundred. OK. Could you sign each cheque there, please?
B: Right.
A: And can I see your passport, please?
B: Yes, certainly. Here you are.
A: Here you are. And your receipt. We take 2% commission, so that's 12,446 pesetas.
B: Er – so what's this coin here?
A: It's a hundred pesetas – that's about eighty cents.
B: Right. Thank you very much.
A: Thank you.

Unit 4 Sound Check. Same spelling ... Exercise 1

export – Asian companies export a lot of electronic goods to Europe.
export – Japanese exports to Europe are very high.

Unit 4 Sound Check. Same spelling... Exercise 2

import, import ; increase, increase; decrease, decrease; transport, transport; contract, contract; produce, produce; extract, extract; insult, insult; progress, progress; contrast, contrast; transfer, transfer; record, record

Unit 4 Sound Check. No stress Exercise 1

manager, worker, shopper, wholesaler, carton, system

Unit 4 Sound Check. No stress Exercise 4

attend, assistant, confirm, recommend, accurate, seasonal

Unit 4 Sound Check. Prefixes... Exercise 1

impatient, inflexible, uneconomic, distasteful, impossible

Unit 4 Sound Check Prefixes... Exercise 2

untidily, improbable, uncommonly, unsympathetic, disagreeable, disappearance

Unit 5A Exercise 3

(organiser)

There are over a thousand exhibitors here from all parts of the world. Most of the big international food and drink companies have taken a stand, and a lot of small ones too. This is a trade exhibition – it's not for members of the public. Manufacturers come here to meet buyers from other companies. It gives buyers and sellers a chance to get to know each other. Exhibitors have brought their new products here, and most of them are doing special promotions to encourage people to buy them. A lot of business is done because everybody knows you can negotiate good discounts. There are lots of events too. Earlier today there was a dragon dance sponsored by a Chinese company, and at midday a West Indian band is playing at the Caribbean food stand. And at a show like this, you don't pay for lunch! Lots of companies are doing cooking demonstrations and tastings, so there are plenty of free samples. It's an important event for anyone in the food industry. Last year's exhibition was very successful, and this year is even better.'

Unit 5B Exercises 3 and 4

(K = Karine, S = Stephen)
K: This is one of our most famous chocolates. It's called 'Caprice'.
S: 'Caprice'?
K: Yes, the filling is made with fresh cream and it's covered with dark chocolate. We sell a lot of Caprice. It's very popular.
S: Well, it looks beautiful. It's a very unusual shape.
K: Yes, we try to make our chocolates look beautiful as well as tasting beautiful. Why don't you taste it?
S: Mmm ... oh yes ... mmm.
K: What do you think?
S: Oh ... it's wonderful ... absolutely delicious ... and it tastes so creamy.

Unit 5C Exercise 6

(S = salesperson, C = customer)
S: Can I help you? Or are you just looking?
C: Er ... well ... I'm looking for a portable.
S: I see. And have you looked at any other machines at the exhibition?
C: Well ... yes, I'm quite impressed by the GATE 166, so I wanted to compare it with this one.
S: Our 166? OK. Well. It's our best-selling machine. It's battery or mains-operated and the battery life is longer than any other machine in its price range – over six hours.
C: Right ... the battery life in the GATE is as long as that.
S: Right ... er ...
C: But what about the hard disk? How big is the hard disk?
S: It comes with a one gigabyte hard disk as standard. It's our fastest machine. It's got a 166 chip in it, as the name suggests.
C: But what about the weight. How heavy is it?
S: Oh, it's very light. Only three and a half kilos.
C: Right. Well, the GATE machine is lighter, then.
S: Yes, just a little, but we're doing a special offer for anyone who buys at the exhibition ... two years' free maintenance and support.
C: Two years ... right. That sounds good.
S: And nobody can beat our price. It's the least expensive machine available with these specifications, at only £1750.
C: Oh ... but isn't the GATE cheaper? They're giving a ten per cent discount for people buying at the exhibition.
S: I see. Well, if you decide to buy our machine, I'm sure we can match their price.

Unit 6B Exercises 2 and 3

(Karine)

We sell loose chocolates in different sizes of ballotin – they are sold by weight, for example, 250 grams, 500 grams. Then we sell a range of boxes of chocolates – our Opera collection is very popular – and a selection of tins. These are decorated ... we have the 1900, the Garden. And we also make napolitains – small flat squares of chocolate that people often eat with a cup of coffee. And of course we make bars of chocolate, we make a lot of different types. We also produce a very small box, or packet, with just two chocolates in it. These are usually sold to catering companies or hotels and airlines who put their own name on the side.

Unit 6B Exercise 9

(Karine)

The customers who buy in our own shops and in the department stores are mainly women.

139

Tapescripts

But in duty-free shops, more and more it's men – people travelling on business. The age of our customers is a little high at the moment. We are obviously targeting people on a good income. City people, people who eat out a lot. At twenty you can't really afford to do that. Now we want to focus on younger people – twenty-five to thirty. We already have a lot of customers around thirty-five to forty, but our main buyers are over fifty.

Unit 6B Exercise 10

(Karine)
People in different countries like their chocolates in different ways. In Germany they like big chocolates; in Britain it's white chocolates that are not too big. In the US the bigger a chocolate is, the better – local US chocolate makers make very big chocolates. In Britain and Europe people want to buy a box of chocolates. In Japan you buy them individually. In Germany you don't buy wrapped luxury chocolates because for Germans wrapped chocolates are cheap – they are not high quality. In our shop in Harrods in London, Arabs ask us to wrap every chocolate individually.
In countries like France and Germany a lot of customers like very dark, bitter chocolates, with a very high percentage of cacao. We introduced the Yucatan for them – a chocolate with 69% cacao and less sugar and milk. In Britain people aren't interested in dark, bitter chocolates. They like chocolates sweet, with a lot of milk.

Unit 6C Exercise 6

(I = interviewer, C = consumer)
1 I: So why do you eat a lot of fast food, then?
  C: Oh, because I leave for work at 7 in the morning and don't get home until about 8 at night. So I often pick up something to eat on the way home ...
2 I: And what about you, madam?
  C: Well, we never seem to be at home at the same times on weekdays. When I get back the children have already gone out. They'll get a sandwich or something if I'm not there ...
3 I: And why do you eat fast food?
  C: Because I live alone and I don't want to spend time cooking for myself ...
4 I: And you, sir?
  C: Er ... because it's quite cheap ... and fast-food places often welcome children and families ... we can all eat out together ... and there are no complaints from the children ...
5 I: And what are your reasons?
  C: I simply haven't got time to cook. If we're not eating fast food from a restaurant, we're probably eating something similar at home ...

Unit 6 Sound Check. Silent letters
Exercise 1

know, knife, knee, knock
write, wrong, wrap, typewriter
campaign, foreign, sign, champagne
would, could, should, calm, talk, walk
comb, lamb, bomb, limb
light, weigh, straight, through

Unit 6 Sound Check. Words with *ough*
Exercise 1

A through
B although, though
C cough
D bought, thought, fought, nought
E rough, tough, enough

Unit 6 Sound Check. 'Missing' syllables
Exercise 1

business, interesting, different, chocolate, temperature, frightening

Unit 7A Exercise 6

(I = interviewer, M = manager)
I: OK. We've already looked at one production process, where you make the centre first and then cover it with chocolate. I can see how that works when the fillings are quite hard, but what about chocolates with soft centres?
M: Yes, that's right. Of course, we can't use the same process with chocolates that have very soft centres – the soft creams and the liqueurs. For these we use what we call the moulding process.
I: So what happens in the moulding process? How is it different?
M: Well, the main difference is that we make the chocolate shells first. After they've been made, we pour the filling into them. The first thing that happens is that liquid chocolate is poured into a tray of moulds. Then the tray is turned over quickly – in this way the extra chocolate falls out and leaves a very thin layer on the sides and bottom of each mould.
I: Ah ... I see; that's how you do it!
M: Yes, it's simple really. Then the moulds are cooled – to make the shells hard – and then we pour in the cream fillings. After the filling has been put in, they go into the cooling tunnel for a second time and then a thin layer of chocolate is put on top of the cream. And finally, after cooling again we take the finished chocolates out of the moulds and pack them by hand.

Unit 7B Exercise 2

Packing is an important part of the production process because it's the packaging that a customer sees first. A good packer in a factory should be able to work quickly and carefully. He or she should be good with their hands ... and in some packing jobs they need to write labels, so a packer should have clear handwriting.

Unit 7C Exercise 5

(Sylvia)
I'll give you an example of a product sheet. Here's the one on the mini-ballotin that we sell a lot of to airlines. It tells you the number of chocolates, which in the mini-ballotin is two. Then there's the total weight ... 33 grams ... that's with the ballotin ... and the weight without the ballotin ... 28 grams. Then the ballotins are packed inside a larger carton for transportation. When you look at this sheet it shows you that each carton holds 84 mini-ballotins. Oh, and the shelf-life – everyone needs to know about that. For these chocolates it's four months. For some of our other ones, with fresh cream, it's one month.

Unit 8A Exercises 3 and 4

(K = Karin)
K: Well ... everything that concerns exports from handling questions from clients to contact with new clients to ... er ... making sure that the orders are passed on to the despatch department, to the invoicing department ... um ... handling everything concerning transport, contacting transport companies ... er ... sending out client information about the flight details for everything ... so everything from A to Z.
K: USA, UK ... um ... Japan, but I'm not dealing with Japan at the moment, that's someone else. Who else? We have a lot of clients in ... um ... in Europe, most of our clients are in Europe ... and we are more and more selling towards the Middle East and the Far East. That's working better and better now.

Unit 8C Exercise 2

(V = visitor, E = Eliane)
V: Hello.
E: Good morning. Can I help you?
V: Er ... I've got an appointment with Karin Thielemans ... at 11.30. I'm a little early.
E: I see. Could I take your name?
V: Yes. It's Alan Walker.
E: And which company are you from, Mr Walker?
V: Sweetman Limited.
E: Sweetman?
V: Yes, that's right.
E: Right. Just a moment, please. I'll call her. (Hello. It's Eliane. I have Mr Walker to see you from Sweetman Limited. ... Yes, OK.) She'll be down in a few minutes, Mr Walker. Would you like to take a seat?
V: Thank you very much.
E: Excuse me ...

Unit 8C Exercise 5

1 (R = receptionist, C = caller)
  R: Good morning. Blane International. Can I help you?
  C: Oh, hello. Er ... Is Jennifer Street there, please?
  R: I'm afraid she's just gone out. She'll be back this afternoon, though.
  C: Ah ...
  R: Would you like to leave her a message?
  C: Er ... well ... yes, I think so.
  R: OK. Just a moment. Right. What message would you like to leave?
  C: Can you ask her to meet me after work ... at 6 o'clock ... er ... in the cafe across the road ... er ... you know ...
  R: The Opera Cafe?
  C: Yes, that's it, the Opera Cafe.
  R: OK. And can I take your name?
  C: Oh yes. It's John Locker.
  R: John Locker ...
2 (R = receptionist, C = caller)
  R: Hello. Blane International. Can I help you?
  C: Yes. My name's Helen Beard, and I've got a meeting with Tom Williams this afternoon at four ...
  R: Yes ...
  C: And I'm calling to cancel it because I'm afraid I'm ill.
  R: Ah, right. I'll pass that on to him. Can I just have your name again, please?
  C: Helen Beard. My number's 652418.
  R: Beard. And your meeting was at four o'clock this afternoon?

C: That's right.
R: Don't worry. I'll let him know.
C: Thanks. Oh, there's one other thing.
R: Yes?
C: Can you tell him I'll put the report in the post. He should get it tomorrow morning.
R: Yes, of course. Thank you for calling.

3 (R = receptionist, C = caller)
R: Good morning. Blane International. How can I help you?
C: Oh, hello Tim, this is Kate ... Kate Allen.
R: Hello Mrs Allen. How are you?
C: Oh, fine thanks. Look, is Peter there?
R: No, I'm afraid he's out at the moment.
C: Oh ... well ... can you ask him to call me? I'm going out right now but I'll be back about two. Could you ask him to call me as soon as possible after that?
R: Certainly, after two o'clock.
C: That's right. See you soon then.

Unit 9A Exercise 2

A: Oh ... I can't stand game shows. I prefer watching concerts and music videos. They're much better.
B: I don't watch any sports programmes ... and there's so much sport on! My favourite programmes are movies – you know, Hollywood films. They're the best.
C: I enjoy comedy programmes, but I prefer the live stand-up shows to sitcoms. Most of those sitcoms are really stupid – especially the American ones.
D: Soap operas always make me turn off. But I watch cartoons a lot.
E: I'm interested in some sports, but I like football better than athletics. And those other ones they call sport ... you know, snooker ... and darts ... I can't stand them. But the worst programmes for me are the talk shows. They're so boring!

Unit 9B Exercise 3

(I = interviewer, R = Iain Renwick)
I: One of the slogans that MTV uses describes an important part of their philosophy. The slogan is, 'Think globally, act locally'. MTV is clearly global – you can watch its programmes all over the world, but how does it try to provide for local needs? What about the language of the programmes, for example?
R: The practical reality is that the international language of music is predominantly English. But in saying that the reflection in our programming content and the content of the channels across the world is driven by the needs of the local markets. So we do have – in Brazil for instance we have a completely Portuguese service. It's language specific. So in south-east Asia we're going language specific – we've got a Mandarin service, we've got an English language service, we've got a Hindi service, we're seeing that developing more in Europe.
I: And what about content? Is the content of MTV programmes the same all over the world?
R: There's obviously a lot of programming that's produced that covers all our channels, and that will be predominantly having been developed in English. So there'll be programming delivered from the European market, from North America that goes into our affiliates throughout the world. But that would be mainly reflected in major award shows – the video music awards in New York, the MTV Europe music awards, the movie awards in LA which MTV does. So there'll always be ... MTV is a global ... it thinks internationally but it can deliver relevance to its local audiences by understanding their preferences but presenting them with the big picture as well, and that's very very important.
One cannot deliver solely with one message for Europe; one has to still clearly, clearly, clearly recognise the cultural diversity and that is to us a huge strength of Europe, is that cultural diversity and that's something that MTV, is reflecting in its structure, in its growing regional structure, in its ability to say yes, we will speak pan-nationally but we'll clearly understand your, your ..., specific requirements, whether it's in Germany, whether it's in Italy, whether it's in the UK.

Unit 9 Sound Check. Words ending in *t* or *d* Exercise 1

a sound, frequent, lost, must
b sound system, frequent flyer, lost luggage, you must be Jill
c product range, department store, trend setter, hand-made

Unit 9 Sound Check. Words ending in *t* or *d* Exercise 2

a chocolate bar, guidebook, good boy, meat packer, that passenger
b I'd been there before.
   It's a hand-made product.
   She's quite poor.

Unit 9 Sound Check. Words ending in *n* Exercise 1

a Eleven people are waiting.
   There's only one passenger.
   I can be there at five.
   I'll see you at the station bookshop.
b Ten passengers have missed the flight.
   He's still in bed.
   She's away on business.
   There's one picture left.

Unit 9 Sound Check. Words ending in *n* Exercise 2

a One pallet holds nine cartons.
   He's an American client.
   I've got a brown coat.
   We can go tomorrow.
b Neuhaus is a Belgian confectioner.
   Please go to the green car park.
   He can get it.
   I've got an Australian guidebook.

Unit 10C Exercise 2

(Vanessa)
My job – I'm mainly responsible for Germany. I also deal with, like, UK and, I don't know, Italy, but the main focus is on Germany. Because I'm German and I know the market, or I should know the market ... know what young people want.
What we do is we get feedback from certain shows. We get the ratings, we get the viewing figures, and then we decide, does that show work in that time slot? Maybe we move it to another time slot ... are we targeting the right audience at the right time with a certain show?
We've got, like, rating figures, or viewing figures over weekdays, Saturdays, Sundays for several months, weeks, whatever, so we plot them and you can see a graph from three o'clock in the morning to three o'clock the next morning and you can see where the peaks and where dips are. So you say OK that's performing well – high viewing figures, high ratings so that's OK. And if you do it for, let's say, weekly for say, four, five, six weeks and you always see at the same time that people are turning off, they're tuning out to watch something else. You think, hang on a minute and you look at this time slot. You look at how this time slot performed a year ago when a different show was on so you can see if it has improved or it's worse.
And, usually when we've got viewing figures, or ratings, or the weekly analysis of how a show's performed ... all that goes to the head of production, and to people who do the scheduling ... er ... music research people when it comes to the music issue.

Unit 11A Exercise 3

(Eva)
Again, I think that in the UK you can develop your career more easily in comparison to other countries. I mean in Germany it is quite normal to stay with a company for er, thirty-five years until you retire ... and you do ... We have this expression, we say you sit it out, you know, you just stay in your job and wait until eventually you get promoted. But this is changing now.
In the UK you get promoted according to how you do the job. It's not so much about your age or how long you've been with a company. People can find jobs where they have a lot more power, a lot more responsibility. And they can earn much higher wages too. But it is hard to work in the UK, you know, working hours are sometimes very long. If you work in sectors like banking ... I know people who work till ten o'clock every night, lots of them, and they work weekends. That is totally crazy, I mean you don't do that in Germany. You might stay late now and then, and you might work the odd weekend, but there are people here that, you know, who don't do anything else except work. Then after ten years they are able to retire; after ten years they are where other people are when they are forty five and they're still only thirty. It is totally different here, totally different.

Unit 11C Exercise 5

(Alison)
You can prepare for interviews and it is possible to improve your interviewing style. The first thing you should do is to find out as much as you can about the company and the job itself. The interviewers will be impressed if you have done some homework on the company. It shows initiative. I always tell people to imagine themselves in the interviewer's situation. What kind of person

are they looking for? How many of those skills and qualities do you have? And how can you demonstrate them as effectively as possible? It is vital to have clear strategies for an interview. How you present yourself is important – the clothes you wear, your body language, the way you speak, how much you smile. You should also look enthusiastic – as if you are really interested in the job. All of these affect an interviewer's decision. The way you speak is particularly important. It is almost always a mistake to talk too much, but speaking too little can also be a problem. You have to be sensitive to the situation. Remember that the interviewer is in control and you should not try to take that control away. But at the same time no interviewer is looking for one-word answers to questions. Most interviewers give you a chance to ask questions at the end, and you should definitely use that opportunity. But again, not too many questions – the interviewers probably only have a few minutes before they need to see someone else!

Unit 11C Exercise 6
(candidate)
Well, first of all I've got quite a lot of experience of the leisure industry. As you know, I've worked in hotels for the last two summers. Er ... and I've had experience of working abroad – one of the hotels was in the south of France, near Nice. I've also got a background in working with young people. You know – from my CV – that I helped to run my local youth club ... and at the hotel last year I managed the reception desk, so I was responsible for the other receptionists.
Then there's my training. I've been studying business management so I understand any business aspects of the job. I'm good with computers. I'm familiar with different software packages ... word-processing, databases and spreadsheets.
My foreign languages are not too bad – I can manage in French and Spanish and I'm learning German.
On the personal side, I think I'm good at working with people ... you know, as part of a team ... but I can also work alone. I'm hard-working ... well-organised ... and enthusiastic ... I know clients can be difficult, but people tell me I'm very diplomatic.

Unit 12A Exercises 2 and 3
(Thomas)
I work as a presenter ... for news. I write them ... I work as a writer as well as a researcher and as a producer on packages, cutting, editing, interviewing ... and so I do the whole sort of newsroom bit ... yeah, I do all round everything basically. There's nothing I don't do there ... so writing, producing, presenting I think would sum it up. I'm basically hired as a presenter and a journalist ... and so journalist functions as well ... without having, sort of, experience as one ... but that's the job.
It's sort of young people's news. So that it works as a news channel for young people. If there's a youth problem or big youth demonstration in Germany we've got the footage of, we'll get the story and that's important news for us. So it's just like ... I think it's like major news except for it's for 15 to 25 year olds. So we don't go for the big international things unless it's involving young people.
We have an editor, we have an editor-in-chief, and then we have a music editor ... the main editor ... we have a morning meeting ... the work procedure is that we meet at nine and go through papers, wires, sources, stories, radio, everything. Ten fifteen we have a morning meeting like a normal news department with ... er ... all come out with our stories and then we discuss them and find out if they're worth taking up. After that we get assigned two or three stories each and ... and from there the day goes on with a deadline at three ... researching and finding the stories and writing them up, or how much is on getting graphics in and everything ...

Unit 13B Exercise 6
(S = Sara, I = interviewer)
S: For a company trying to do business on the Internet, the design of your Web site is extremely important. And when I talk about design I don't just mean producing something that looks nice. A site is well-designed if it works ... that is, it does three key things. First of all it attracts people to look at it – without that you've failed. The second is that it keeps the viewer interested ... keeps them coming back for more visits. And finally, the purpose of all company Web sites at the end of the day ... it must help you sell your product or your service. All company Web sites try to achieve these three aims.
I: So how can you design a Web site so that people want to keep visiting it?
S: Well ... the introductory page is important. So many companies just put pages on the Web and leave them there. If you look at it in December you find it hasn't changed at all since six months earlier. You must maintain a Web site, and one of the best ways of encouraging repeat visits is to keep changing the introductory page – provide up-to-date information, focus on different products, give visitors something new to see and do. I mean, it's a bit like a newspaper – when you've read a newspaper once you don't go back and have another look at it the following week, do you? We want to read about something different. It's the same with a Web site.
I: What about the content of a Web site? What general advice can you give to someone setting up a Web site for the first time?
S: Good Web sites are separated into different pages. Every page should, of course, contain the company name and a way of contacting them. It should also provide a list of what is available on the other pages and an easy way of moving from one page to another ... maybe some sort of map of the site where you can click on the other pages.
I: OK, but what about the actual information on the site?
S: Well, let's take an example. A record company, for instance. It will have information about the company's products – a catalogue of some sort. It may have a group of pages that provides background information on its artists. It may allow you to listen to particular pieces of music and perhaps see video clips. It will certainly have a contact page, which allows you to e-mail the company and perhaps order its products. They may even have a chatline, a forum that allows you to ask questions to your favourite star and . perhaps even get replies. There could be quizzes, competitions, special offers. There's no limit, really.

Unit 14A Exercise 3
(Björn)
What we have done so far is that we have made up our own environmental policy. We look at how we use, for example, energy, how we sit when we work, what we use for chemicals, how we transport people, how we transport films – everything. And what we try to do is to set goals for causing less environmental damage. So we make the right choice every time we have to, for instance, decide about transport – to transport by train or by bicycle, and so on. We write down how we do things today and what our goals are for the next year. We have already made some changes. For instance, we use a lot of chemicals and plastic film in our reproduction process, and now we have new green film which is less hard on the environment and the chemicals we use are recycled. We choose print companies that do not use harmful, poisonous colours. We employ a consultant to drive this project and she helps us to ask the right questions. We do this because we care about our environment, but it's also very important for our relationship with customers. And we look at how our partners work – do they have an environmental policy? If they don't, we can't work with them.

Unit 14A Exercise 6
(consultant)
We're here today to talk about business and the environment. Well, every company needs to consider the following three key areas. Firstly, input – in other words, the resources that we use ... the things we need to do our work, to make products or provide services. Secondly, the process, or what we do with those resources in the workplace – the way we use them. And lastly, the output from our business – and by output I mean the products and waste materials that are the results of our work.
So what can we do to cause as little damage as possible to the environment? Well, we can look at the things we buy and see if there are better alternatives. If there are, then we need to persuade suppliers to provide them. And they may be able to use less packaging too, if we ask them to.
Next, within our workplaces, we need to use our resources efficiently, so there's no waste. We can, for example, switch off office machines that are not in use, and we can make sure that delivery vans only leave when they are full.
Then, output. Well, how much waste is really necessary? We must ask ourselves if it's recyclable. Or could another company use it as a raw material for its products? If these options are not possible, then we must dispose of the waste safely.

Unit 14B Exercise 2

(A = Anne, P = Peter, L = Len, C = Carol)

A: Right, let's start then. Maggie Price sends her apologies – she's got a meeting with a client. You know Carol Pearson, my secretary, don't you?
P: Yes, of course.
L: Hello, Carol.
A: Carol's kindly agreed to take minutes of our meetings. So, the first point on the agenda concerns the appointment of an environmental consultant. The board's agreed that we need outside help from a specialist to look at our work practices and suggest improvements. So we need to approach a suitable person or organisation. Len, I think you've been taking care of that?
L: Yes, there are four local organisations that could help. Er ... they're called Business Care, Green Alert, Efficient Living and Our Earth. I've spoken briefly to all of them and Green Alert seems by far the most professional. Their fees seem reasonable too, so I suggest we start by speaking to them in a bit more depth.
P: I know Mary Hill, who works there, quite well.
A: OK, well why don't we ask Mary Hill to our next meeting. Peter will you contact her?
P: Yes, fine.
A: But we should make it clear that it's only to talk about her possible involvement in helping us set environmental goals – no commitment. OK, let's move on. Point two ... keeping colleagues informed about what we're doing. Very important if we want them to feel part of the changes that are going to be made.
L: And we should have some way of asking them for their opinions and ideas too.
A: Yes, of course. Now, how shall we do that?
L: Well, we could copy the minutes of these meetings to them.
A: Well, the directors certainly want copies. Carol, can you arrange that?
C: Yes, right.
P: Why don't we do a chatty news-sheet for everyone else? We could use it to make people aware about environmental issues as well as what we're doing in this group. I haven't got a lot of time myself, though.
A: Well, I'd be happy to do it, with Carol's help... if the directors agree that I can do it in company time. We'll need some money for it too. I'll bring a sample news-sheet to our next meeting if they approve. And I'll have calculated the cost by next Wednesday's directors' meeting. So let's go on to our last point ... finances. Len, you were going to talk to John and Penny.
L: Yes, I did. They really want Vision Design to be seen as a green company, so they know that there'll be costs involved in an environmental policy – including the cost of staff time. They do want to know what those costs are likely to be before we start spending anything, though, and of course they will hire the consultant themselves after we make a proposal to them.
A: Fine, right, well we need to meet this Mary Hill first. So let's just agree on future meetings. Is everyone happy with Tuesdays?
P: Hmm. They're difficult for me. Would Thursday be possible? 4.30?
L: No problem for me.
A: Yes, that's fine. Shall we make it the second Thursday in each month?
L: Fine.
P: Yes, good.
A: So the next meeting's on January 14th. Right. Oh, well, thanks for coming.

Unit 14B Exercise 7

(S = Sam, J = John, P = Penny)

S: Right, let's start. Patrick will be taking the minutes as usual. Now, I asked Anne Byron to join us, but she's been called away suddenly on a personal matter. Let's see, yes, the first item of business is new staff. How is Pam doing, John?
J: Well, I'm a bit worried about her, actually, Sam. She's got a real problem with punctuality – she was nearly an hour late yesterday. I've spoken to her, but we'll have to see.
S: Hmm. And you've been interviewing for a new secretary, Penny?
P: Yes, I'll have seen everyone by the end of this week, so I'll bring the files of the best three to next week's meeting and we can make a decision.
S: Anything else on new staff? No? Good. Let's move on, then. Environmental policy. Anne has left me some notes ... yes. As you know from their minutes, the Environmental Group met on December 8th, and they have now contacted Mary Hill. She's agreed to attend their next meeting, and then we'll decide whether to hire her. We'll wait for the group's proposal before we discuss finances, but Anne has asked for £1,500 a year to produce a news-sheet for all staff. It will also take four hours of her time each month and a day of Carol's time. Any comments?
P: No, I think that sounds reasonable.
J: Yes, why don't we agree to that for six months initially, and review it at the end of that period.
S: Agreed. Then there's only one more important issue this week, which you raised, Penny, and that's parking.
P: Ah, yes, the car park is so crowded now that clients can't park there – and of course there's no parking on the street outside. I've done an informal survey, and about 80% of our staff come to work in their own car...
J: ... which is ridiculous, when we're so near the station and there's a bus stop on the corner. Some of them should share cars – as Penny and I do. This might be a good subject for Anne's first news-sheet. She could explain the problem for clients and for the environment. Then she could suggest alternatives to using cars.
S: An excellent idea. Will you speak to her, then, John?
J: Certainly.
S: Right. Anything else?
P: Oh, can we start the meeting slightly later next week? I've got to be in London and I won't be back until three.
S: That's fine with me – three thirty, then? John?
J: Fine.
S: OK. Let's close this meeting, then. Are you playing tennis this evening, Penny?

Unit 15A Exercise 1

(Jacob)

I don't actually work with interactive media at Intra, although I have the skills – I work on the design of print materials like brochures. I do use the Internet a lot, though, and of course I need English for that. I look for well-designed Web sites and study the typefaces and so on – that's a professional interest. Then I shop on the Internet, read about music, and look for particular information. There's a frightening amount of information out there, and like all media you can't believe everything you read, but as far as I'm concerned the Internet's a tool, a quick way of finding something I need.

Unit 15. Sound Check. Emphasising ... Exercise 1

Shall we get them a T-shirt each?
John would like a T-shirt but I think Kate would prefer some chocolates.

Oh, that's absolutely wonderful!
Well I would prefer to go home now.

Unit 15. Sound Check. Emphasising ... Exercise 2

A: Can I help you?
B: Yes. Do you sell children's clothes?
A: No, I'm afraid we only sell clothes for adults.

Unit 15. Sound Check. Rising and falling ... Exercise 1

The factory's near Moscow.
The factory's near Moscow?
The factory's near Moscow ...

Unit 15. Sound Check. Rising and falling ... Exercise 2

A: I'm going to visit that company in Paris.
B: You are?
A: The boss wants me to collect some things ...
B: Things?
A: You know, some brochures, a few samples and he wants a price list.

Unit 16A Exercise 5

(secretary)

There are some things I won't do because I just think they're insulting. I won't clean the office and it's not my job to keep the plants alive. I'm not a cleaner and I'm not a servant – I'm a secretary and personal assistant. I'll make coffee for my boss sometimes, but he also makes coffee for me. Well, that's fine. But I don't want him to think he can treat me like a servant. In general I'll do anything that's important for the company's business. I'll look after the clients in the day, and sometimes I'll take them out to dinner in the evening. I'll even go shopping to buy gifts for clients, but I won't do any personal shopping for my boss. When my boss asks me to do anything, I always think – would he ask me to do this if I were a man? If the answer's yes then I'll probably do it.

Unit 16B Exercise 3

(trainer)

Staff in Customer Services have one main goal, and that is to make sure that every customer that comes to see you leaves feeling satisfied. You'll meet many different types of people and you will need different strategies for dealing with each.

143

Tapescripts

The most difficult customers are the ones who are angry. They behave aggressively ... they shout ... and sometimes they may even threaten you. It's easy to get angry yourself in these situations, but believe me, that's a big mistake. Your first job is to calm the customer down and the best way to do this is to let the customer speak while you try to show that you understand, and sympathise with the problem. The second group of customers I want to mention are those who are confused. Many customers find it difficult to explain their problem. This might be because they don't understand something – about a product ... or about payment, or something like that; it might be because they're elderly ... or perhaps they're just nervous. It's surprising how nervous some people can be in these situations. Whatever the reason, some people find it difficult to be clear about what exactly is wrong and how you can help. With people like this the important thing is to ask questions to clarify the problem ... and to guide the customer into explaining what they want. It's important to spend time with this kind of customer.

Then there are those who I call the 'talkers' – the ones who just seem to have come for a conversation and have all the time in the world. They have some reason for being there, but they're more interested in chatting to you endlessly. The best strategy with this kind of customer is to be polite but firm in dealing with the problem and to move the conversation along and bring it to a close. For example, you might say 'Thank you for your valuable comments. I don't want to take up any more of your time.'

Fortunately, most people who come to Customer Services just want information, and on these occasions all you need to do is answer their questions in a polite, friendly and efficient way.

Unit 16B Exercise 4

(C = customer, A = assistant)
C: Is this where I make a complaint?
A: This is Customer Services. Can I help you?
C: Are you the manager? I demand to see the manager immediately!
A: He's not here at the moment, I'm afraid. Can I help you?
C: Look, I've phoned several times already and nothing's happened. I'm not leaving until this is sorted out.
A: All right, there's no need to get angry! Just tell me what the problem is.
C: Don't you speak to me like that. I've got good reason to be angry and I won't be spoken to in that tone of voice.
A: I'm not speaking to you in any tone of voice. I'm just trying to find out what the problem is.
C: Well, I'll tell you. I've got a maintenance contract with this company on my computer ... a very expensive maintenance contract if you ask me ... and it says that if my computer goes wrong, someone will come to my house within 24 hours and repair it.
A: Yes ...
C: Well ... four days ago I phoned this place and I spoke to someone and told them I needed an engineer to come and look at it. Nobody came. The next day I called again and you promised me the engineer would call. Nothing. For the next two days I called every half hour, but the phone was engaged all day. It's now four days later and still nothing has happened. Now I've had to drive twenty miles today to find out what's going on. It's unbelievable, the whole thing. I've paid for a contract and when something goes wrong I expect some service. Now what are you going to do?
A: I can't believe our lines were engaged all day ...
C: Are you calling me a liar? How dare you ...
A: Look, just give me your name and address, will you?
C: I can't believe this. You fail to provide a service I've paid for. I come here and all I get is rudeness.
A: You're the one who's being rude.

Unit 16C Exercise 3

(S = secretary, C = caller)
S: Good morning, Blackwood Copiers. Can I help you?
C: Hello. I'm phoning to complain about your maintenance service.
S: I see. Can I take your name, please sir?
C: My name? It's Peter England.
S: And the company name, Mr England?
C: I'm phoning from Take Two Limited. I'm the office manager.
S: Take Two. Thank you, Mr England. Right. Could you tell me exactly what the problem is?
C: Yes. We had one of your maintenance men here three days ago to repair a photocopier. He came and had a look at the machine and said it needed a new spare part. He didn't have the part with him but promised to come and fit it the next day. That was three days ago and nothing has happened. We've now been without a copier for nearly a week and it's making my life very difficult ... and making me very angry.
S: I understand how you feel, Mr England. I'm terribly sorry about the delay. I'll do everything I can to sort things out.
C: Well ... look ... I know it's not your fault ...
S: Don't worry, I know delays like this cause a lot of problems. So, the problem is that your photocopier is not working and you need it repaired urgently.
C: Yes. Exactly.
S: Right. Could you give me the repair order details, please, and I'll check on the computer.
C: Yes. The reference number I was given is 40598 and the date your technician was ... er .. it was on Monday ... er ... that was March 5th.
S: OK. Just a moment. I'm just calling it up on the screen. Right. Here it is. Take Two, 26 High Street, Cambridge. Is that right?
C: Yes, that's it.
S: OK. I'm just reading what it says. Right. Yes. I'm afraid the part you needed was out of stock on Monday.
C: Out of stock! It can't have been out of stock! He phoned from my office to check that it was available!
S: I apologise, Mr England. This does seem to be our fault. Somebody here must have made a mistake.
C: I just can't believe it. He phoned from my office, gave them the part number he needed ... oh ... what's the point. Well thank you for the apology, anyway. So what happens now? When am I going to get the copier repaired?
S: Right. I'll see what I can do. The spare part is now in stock and I'll arrange for our technician to come to you immediately. He can be with you in about an hour's time, by about 11 o'clock.
C: Is that definite?
S: Absolutely certain.
C: Well, 11 o'clock would be fine.
S: Good. And let me apologise once again, Mr England. If you have any problems in future, just call and ask for me. My name's Sally Oak and I'm at Customer Services.
C: Right. Thank you for your help.
S: That's all right, Mr England. I'll call you in a few hours to check that the repair has been done.
C: OK. Let me give you a number where you can reach me this morning. Er ... 351782 ... you should get me on that number.
S: 351782. Fine.
C: Thanks again. Goodbye.
S: Goodbye, Mr England.

Learning Skills. Learning new words
Exercise 1

(T = teacher F = Friederike)
T: So, Friederike, how do you go about learning new words?
F: Well, I use this system that I learnt from a colleague at work. We were talking about how we learn vocabulary, he's taking French classes at the moment, and he told me about this really interesting technique that he'd been taught at school.
T: How does it work?
F: Um, it's all based on cards.
T: Cards?
F: Yes, cards. You see, during a lesson or when I'm reading something like a book or newspaper, I write down 10 words which I think are really important or useful.
T: Or that you like?
F: Yes, or that I like. Then next, I check what they mean in my dictionary and if I still think they're useful ...
T: Or that you still like them?
F: Yes! Then I write them on separate pieces of paper, with the word on one side and the definition and an example sentence on the other.
T: For example?
F: Well, say I've found the word 'annoying'.
T: Yes ...
F: Right. I write 'annoying' on one side of the card and then its meaning, for example, 'another word for irritating' on the other side with a sentence. So, for example, 'I find it very annoying when people smoke in my house because I hate cigarette smoke.'
T: Right, I see now.
F: And then I carry the cards around with me in my bag and test myself when I'm on the bus, wherever. Sometimes I put them on the fridge door in the kitchen!
T: So that you always see them.
F: Yes. Then when I think I know them, I write them in other example sentences or try to use them in class. Then I put them in a box. When I've got 100 words in the box, I test myself again and throw away the ones I can remember. It's very satisfying!

144